GOING FOR GOLD

GAIN ACCESS TO THE GOLD AND SILVER VAULT OF KNOWLEDGE INCLUDING:

- GOLD AND SILVER BUYING / SELLING 101
- THE HISTORY OF MONEY
- THE FUTURE OF MONEY
- THE COLLAPSE OF THE DOLLAR & MORE...

ANDREW SORCHINI

WITH
CLAY CLARK

Disclaimer: Throughout the pages of this book, many trusted experts are quoted and referenced. The appearance of a quote from a trusted expert does not in any way indicate their endorsement of Beverly Hills Precious Metals.

Going For Gold

ISBN 979-8-9899482-1-5

Published by Clay Clark Publishing 2026 | 3920 W 91st St. Tulsa, OK, 74132

NOTABLE QUOTABLE

"If you don't own Gold, you know neither history nor economics."

RAY DALIO

(Raymond Thomas Dalio (born August 8, 1949) is an American billionaire and hedge fund manager, who has been co-chief investment officer of Bridgewater Associates since 1985. As of December 2024, Dalio ranks #124 on Forbes' Richest People in the World with a net worth of $15.4 billion. He founded Bridgewater in 1975 in his New York City two-bedroom apartment. Dalio was born in New York City and attended C.W. Post College of Long Island University before receiving an MBA from Harvard Business School in 1973.)

Have you ever wondered why the price of gold has gone from $35 per ounce in 1971 to over $5,000 per ounce in 2026? Have you ever wondered why the purchasing price of everything goes up year after year? Have you ever wondered where money comes from? If you have ever wanted to know the answers to these questions, then this book was written for you!

This book was created to provide you with the ULTIMATE guide to owning and investing in gold and silver while providing you with a POWERFUL OVERVIEW of the history and the future (or lack thereof) of the United States dollar.

Andrew Sorchini speaks at Clay Clark & General Flynn's ReAwaken America Tour featuring Eric Trump, Mike Lindell, General Flynn, Jim Breuer, Amanda Grace, Julie Green, Pastor Dave Scarlett and countless well-known conservative leaders and experts.

U.S. MONEY SUPPLY (1959-2026):

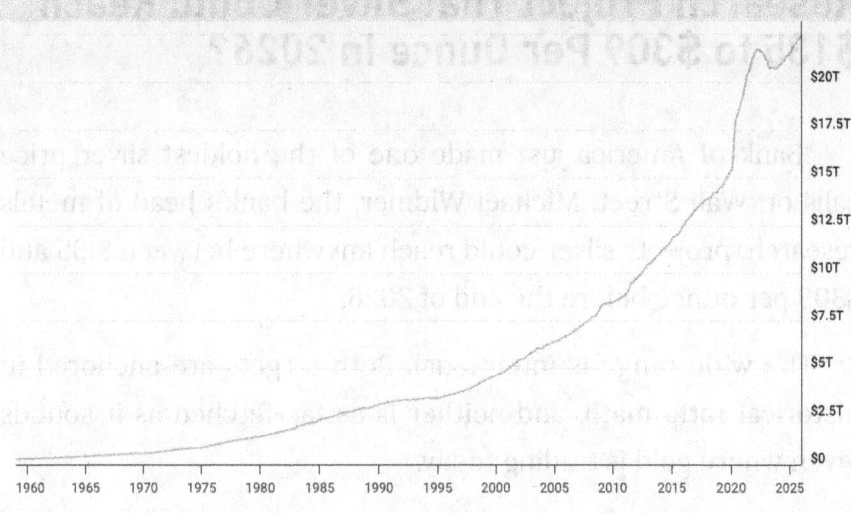

(M2 Money Supply (1959-2026), MacroTrends.net)

PRICE OF GOLD SINCE 1971:

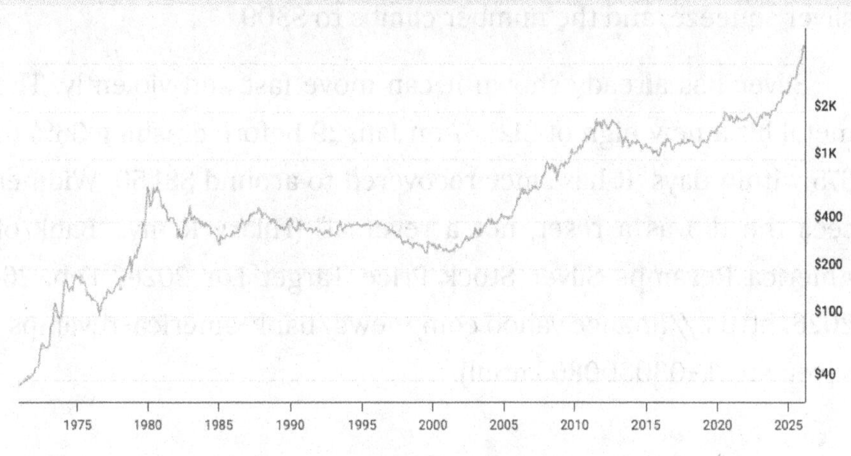

(Gold Prices - 100 Year Historical Chart, MacroTrends.net)

For more information on the graphs above relating to the correlation of the United States cash flow and the price of gold, visit MacroTrends.net.

Why Did Bank of America' Head of Metals Research Project That Silver Could Reach $135 to $309 Per Ounce In 2026?

"Bank of America just made one of the boldest silver price calls on Wall Street. Michael Widmer, the bank's head of metals research, projects silver could reach anywhere between $135 and $309 per ounce before the end of 2026.

The wide range is intentional. Both targets are anchored in historical ratio math, and neither is as far-fetched as it sounds given where gold is trading today.

The math behind both targets starts with the gold-to-silver ratio, currently sitting at roughly 59:1. With gold near $5,000, applying the 2011 ratio low of 32:1 puts silver at $135. Apply the 1980 extreme of 14:1, the level reached during the Hunt Brothers silver squeeze, and the number climbs to $309.

Silver has already shown it can move fast and violently. The metal hit a new high of $121.67 on Jan. 29 before crashing 36% to $75 within days. It has since recovered to around $81.50. Widmer sees the dip as a reset, not a reversal" (Hilary Remy, "Bank of America Revamps Silver Stock Price Target For 2026," Feb. 26, 2026, https://finance.yahoo.com/news/bank-america-revamps-silver-stock-030300865.html).

TABLE OF CONTENTS

CHAPTER 01

Gold & Silver Protect Wealth
Because They Have Both A
Monetary and Industrial Value **9**

CHAPTER 02

Owning Gold & Silver Allows You To
Have Tangible Assets That Do Not
Have Counterparty Risks............................**61**

CHAPTER 03

Liquid Assets Such As Gold Allow
You To Be Financially Malleable...............**83**

CHAPTER 04

Dollars Decrease In Value While
Gold & Silver Increase In Value.................**121**

The national debt of the United States is now at $39 trillion as of the time that this book is being written. Why does this matter to you and I? Every time the United States prints money that it does not have to buy things that it cannot afford to appease voters, corporations, lobbyists and any group of people, our money is becoming worth less. Year after year as our money is becoming exponentially worth less it shall eventually become "worthless." To provide some context and some urgency related to your need to protect your wealth against wealth-destroying inflation I want you to consider the following mind-blow information listed below:

AS OF 2026, THE UNITED STATES NATIONAL DEBT EQUALS $357,068 PER TAXPAYER.

The graph below depicts the United States national debt as of the end of 2025.

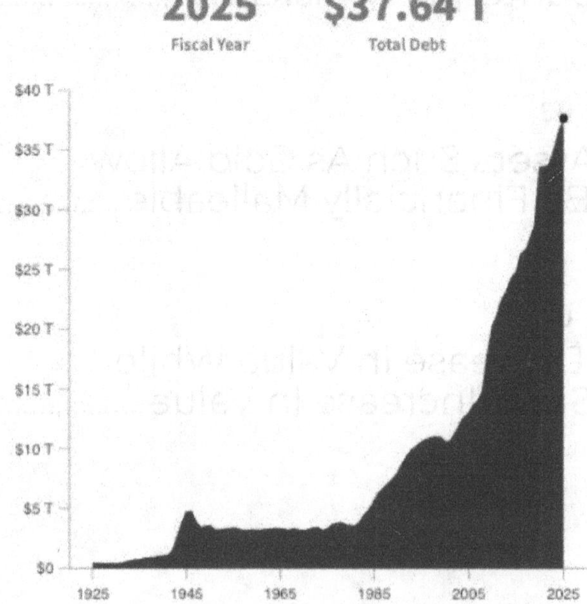

Visit the Historical Debt Outstanding dataset to explore and download this data. The inflation data is sourced from the Bureau of Labor Statistics.

Last Updated: September 30, 2025

CHAPTER 01

G

Gold & Silver Protect Wealth Because They Have Both A Monetary and Industrial Value

Ultimately, we believe that when it comes to building up wealth and improving your net worth you must sincerely view your time as your most important asset because you can usually make more money, but you can't make more time. However, once you begin to earn money as a result of being a world-class employee or business owner, it is very important for you to learn how to get your money to work for you. You need to view your money as an employee that is willing to work for you 24 hours per day, but you must learn how to direct your money. You must learn how to direct your money into assets that will increase in value over time even as the United States dollar loses value.

NOTABLE QUOTABLE

"You don't get paid for the hour. You get paid for
the value you bring to the hour."

JIM ROHN

*(Jim Rohn (1930 – 2009) was an American entrepreneur, author, and
motivational speaker. Jim Rohn mentored Mark R. Hughes and life
strategist Tony Robbins in the late 1970s. Others who credit Rohn for
influencing their careers include authors and lecturers such as Mark
Victor Hansen and Jack Canfield (Chicken Soup book series), Everton
Edwards (Hallmark Innovators Conglomerate), Brian Tracy, Darren
Hardy, and Harv Eker. Rohn coauthored the novel Twelve Pillars with
Chris Widener. Find Jim's work on the Jim Rohn Motivation Youtube
Channel.)*

Who Is This Book Written For?

- This book is written for conservative investors who are
  looking to protect their wealth, and to prevent their hard-
  earned money from being worth nothing as a result of
  the excessive-government-spending- caused inflation.

- This book is written for people who are looking to learn
  everything they need to know about currency, money,
  gold, and silver in under 2 hours.

- This book is written for people who don't mind
  occasionally laughing while learning.

Why Did We Write This Book?

- We wrote this book to produce the world's most effective and informative gold and silver buying guidebook.

- We wrote this book to produce a power-packed and action-item filled gold and silver guidebook that you can read within two hours.

- We wrote this book to teach you everything that you need to know in order to protect your wealth against inflation by investing in gold and silver.

- We wrote this book to both entertain and educate while learning a life-changing approach to building and storing wealth.

- We wrote this book to remove the stress that you may experience as it relates to buying and selling gold and silver because unfortunately, many people find money to be a core source of consistent stress.

FUN FACTS:

- » 70% of Americans are feeling financially stressed, a new CNBC survey finds.

- » 84% figure from a NerdWallet study (2024 Financial Angst Report) shows that a large majority of Americans experience significant financial stress, primarily due to rising costs for food, housing, and insufficient savings, highlighting a widespread issue that financial literacy and open money conversations can help manage.

Who Is Andrew Sorchini?

Andrew Sorchini is founder of Beverly Hills Precious Metals. Andrew Sorchini's involvement in gold and silver started over 30 years ago at his first job in Los Angeles, CA. After many years in the markets and collecting precious metals privately, Andrew opened Beverly Hills Precious Metals Exchange in 2010 to bring precious metals to the homes of Americans.

Over the years, Andrew Sorchini has been referenced as the recommended precious metal detailer of choice for Peter Navarro, General Flynn, Kash Patel, Mel K, Amanda Grace, Pastor Dave Scarlett, Clay Clark, Lara Trump and other leading conservative voices. Andrew is a regular at Clay Clark and General Michael Flynn's Reawaken America Tour, and is actively involved in carrying the mission of the benefits of owning precious metals to various ministries via podcasts.

He has been a frequent guest on Clay Clark's ThriveTime Show, His Glory Show with Pastor Dave Scarlett, The Mel K Show, and Arc of Grace with Amanda Grace.

Contact Andrew Sorchini

Phone: (866) 346-5325

Email: Andrew@BH-PM.com

Fax: (888) 415-6369

Mail Address: Beverly Hills Precious Metals Exchange, Inc. 9663 Santa Monica Blvd. Suite 811 Beverly Hills, CA 90210

Who Is Clay Clark?

Clay Clark is the co-founder of five children, the organizer, emcee and host of the General Flynn ReAwaken America Tour (www. TimeToFreeAmerica.com), the former "U.S. SBA Entrepreneur of the Year" for the State of Oklahoma, the founder of several multi-million dollar companies. Clay Clark's ThrivetimeShow. com podcast has been number one overall on the iTunes business podcast charts 6 times. Clay Clark is a member of the Forbes Business Coach Council, an Amazon best-selling author and the host of The Thrivetime Show podcast. As a musician Clay Clark has produced and released nearly 100 songs which you can find on Spotify and he is a best-selling author of 40+ books. Throughout his career, Clay Clark has purchased hundreds of chickens (for his hobby farm) and he has founded several successful businesses and organizations including:

- www.DJConnection.com

- www.EpicPhotos.com

- www.EITRLounge.com

- www.MakeYourLifeEpic.com

- Party Perfect (Which Clay Clark Grew And Sold)

- The Tulsa Bridal Association Wedding Show

- TipTopK9 Franchising (Clay Clark did not start TipTopK9 Dog Training, he co-founded TipTopK9 Franchising)

- The Tulsa Bridal Association Wedding Show

Throughout his career, he has been featured in Fast Company, Bloomberg, Forbes, Entrepreneur Magazine, PandoDaily, and numerous other publications. He's been the speaker and consultant of choice for top brands throughout the country including: Hewlett Packard, Maytag University, Valspar Paint, and O'Reilly's Auto Parts. Clay is also the co-founder of 5 children, and is the proud owner of thousands of trees, dozens of chickens, and 13 cats.

Clay's Thrivetime Show podcast has featured the following guests and more:

Past Interviews & Headlines:

 8x New York Times Best-Selling Author and Leadership Expert, **John Maxwell**

 Celebrity Chef, Entrepreneur, and New York Times Best-Selling Author, **Wolfgang Puck**

 Legendary Former Key Apple Employee Turned Venture Capitalist, Best Selling Author, **Guy Kawasaki**

 New York Times Best-Selling Co-Author of *Rich Dad Poor Dad*, **Sharon Lechter**

 Senior Pastor of the Largest Church in America with Over 100,000 Weekly Attendees (Lifechurch.tv), **Craig Groeschel**

 One of America's Most Trusted Financial Experts and Has Written Nine Consecutive New York Times Bestsellers with 7 million+ Books in Print, **David Bach**

 Legendary Conservative Strategist, **Roger Stone**

 NBA Hall of Famer, **David Robinson** (2-time NBA Champion, 2-time Gold Medal Winner)

 Senior Editor for Forbes and 3x Best-Selling Author, **Zack O'Malley Greenburg**

 Most Downloaded Business Podcaster of All-Time (EOFire.com), **John Lee Dumas**

 The 25th U.S. National Security Advisor and Retired U.S. Army General, **General Michael Flynn**

 New York Times Best-Selling Author of *Purple Cow*, and former Yahoo! Vice President of Marketing, **Seth Godin**

 Co-Founder of the 700+ Employee Advertising Company (AdRoll), **Adam Berke**

 Emmy Award-winning Producer of the *Today Show* and New York Times Best-Selling Author of *Sh*tty Moms*, **Mary Ann Zoellner**

 New York Times Best-Selling Author of Contagious: *Why Things Catch On* and Wharton Business Professor, **Jonah Berger**

 New York Times Best-Selling Author of *Made to Stick* and Duke University Professor, **Dan Heath**

 International Best-Selling Author of In Search of Excellence, **Tom Peters**

 NBA Player and Coach, **Muggsy Bogues** (Shortest player to ever play in the league)

 NFL Running Back, **Rashad Jennings** (and Winner of Dancing with the Stars)

Lee Cockerell (The former Executive Vice President of Walt Disney World who once managed 40,000 employees)

Michael Levine (PR consultant of choice for Michael Jackson, Prince, Nike, Charlton Heston, Nancy Kerrigan, etc.)

Billboard Contemporary Christian Top 40 Recording Artist, **Colton Dixon**

Conservative Talk Pundit, Frequent Fox News Contributor, Political Commentator and Best-Selling Author, **Ben Shapiro**

See additional guests at Thrivetimeshow.com

What Is Money?

- According to Merriam-Webster, money is defined as "Something generally accepted as a medium of exchange, a measure of value, or a means of payment: such as officially coined or stamped metal currency."

- Money is a standard of value which is at a generally agreed-upon measurement used to express the price of goods and services.

- Money is a way to store value, which is thus capable of holding and maintaining purchasing power over vast periods of time. Money allows people to save value and to thereby defer their spending of their hard-earned money until some future date.

- Money is a trusted medium of exchange, which can easily and reliably be transferred from one person to another person in exchange for goods and services.

What Is Sound Money?

The phrase known as "sound money" comes from the literal and clear ringing sound ("sound") that is made when real gold, silver and copper coins are dropped on a hard surface. This sound can be contrasted with the sound of debased or counterfeit coins that would make dull thud sounds.

Figuratively "sound money" is money that people, countries, businesses and humanity trusts because it exists in a limited supply and is thus, by definition, not subject to government manipulation. However, fiat currencies (currencies issued via decree that are backed by nothing but the faith and trust people have in a system) are controlled and often weaponized by governments, which have been proven to be consistently and fundamentally incapable of managing their monetary affairs.

"Blessed are the young for they shall inherit the national debt."

PRESIDENT HERBERT HOOVER

(Herbert Clark Hoover (August 10, 1874 – October 20, 1964) was the 31st president of the United States, serving from 1929 to 1933. A wealthy mining engineer before his presidency, Hoover led the wartime Commission for Relief in Belgium and was the director of the U.S. Food Administration, followed by post-war relief of Europe. As a member of the Republican Party, he served as the third United States secretary of commerce from 1921 to 1928 before being elected president in 1928. His presidency was dominated by the Great Depression, and his policies and methods to combat it were seen as inadequate and overly conservative. Amid his unpopularity, he decisively lost reelection to the socialist-leaning Franklin D. Roosevelt in 1932.)

NOTABLE QUOTABLE

"Central banks and finance ministries do not hold
copper, aluminum, or steel supplies, yet they hold
gold. The only explanation for central bank gold
hoards is the obvious one - gold is money."

JAMES G. RICKARDS

*(James G. Rickards is the author of The Road to Ruin: The Global
Elites' Secret Plan for the Next Financial Crisis. James G. Rickards is
an American lawyer, economist, investment banker, speaker, media
commentator, and author on matters of finance and precious metals.
He graduated from Johns Hopkins University in 1973 with a Bachelor
of Arts degree with honors, and in 1974, from the Paul H. Nitze School
of Advanced International Studies in Washington, D.C., with an
M.A. in international economics. He received his Juris Doctor from
the University of Pennsylvania Law School and a Master of Laws in
taxation from New York University School of Law. He has held senior
positions at Citibank, Long-Term Capital Management, and Caxton
Associates. Rickards worked on Wall Street for 35 years.)*

When Did Gold Start to Be Used As a Form of Currency?

Over the time and throughout the centuries humans on the
planet earth have tried to use an incredible variety of things to
use as money. In fact, we know that the ancient Egyptians used
barley as a form of money; we know that the Tibetans were using
bricks made out of compressed tea leaves (that they would then
cut pieces off to make change); and we also know that pretty
much every society on the planet has used livestock as a medium
of exchange and a form of money (goats, cows, slaves, and more).

However, nearly every kind of money that humanity tried to use did not work for a variety of reasons. When seashells were used it turned out that they were too fragile, and supply of seashells would exponentially increase after a ravaging storm (inflation). Goats were always interchangeable, and they were not able to hold their value over time. Thus after centuries of testing out different forms or currency, most advanced societies decided to settle on the use of some form of metal to be their money. Metal was more durable than a cow and less likely to be inflated like seashells. Metals such as copper, silver, bronze and gold were then mined out of the earth and turned into coins that were commonly recognized. These coins could be produced in an almost identical way where they could then be stored, traded and exchanged. Bronze and copper started out as being the most common form of money. Over time silver began to be used as money, however, beautiful and hard to find gold became the most coveted and prized form of money overall.

Many historians believe that the first true coins made of gold appeared in Lydia, which is now a part of present-day Turkey, and is also known as Gomar in the Bible. The first gold coins started being used in Turkey around the year 600 B.C.. Over time, the use of gold coins spread among the Greeks, Romans and Persians as improved techniques for minting and refining gold were developed.

NOTABLE QUOTABLE

"If I have cash and I can't figure a way to put it into real estate or my business, I hold it in gold and silver."

ROBERT KIYOSAKI

(Robert Kiyosaki is an international best-selling author of the Rich Dad Poor Dad book series, a legendary real estate investor, multiple-time ThrivetimeShow.com podcast guest, and entrepreneur. Kiyosaki is the author of more than 26 books, including the international self-published personal finance Rich Dad Poor Dad series of books which has been translated into 51 languages and sold over 41 million copies worldwide.)

What Is Fiat Currency & Fiat Money?

- The word fiat is Latin for "let it be done" or "via a formal authorization or decree."

- Fiat currency is the current government-issued currency used in America. Fiat currency is money that is not backed by a physical commodity like gold. However, fiat currency is money that is backed by the trust and faith that people have in the government that issues the currency. As long as people have trust and faith in the government that is issuing the money, the currency will then maintain its value. The word "fiat" is Latin for "let it be done," reflecting its authoritative creation by a government decree. The most common examples of fiat currency currently in use include the U.S. dollar, euro, and Japanese yen.

NOTABLE QUOTABLE

"Gold is the world's least understood asset class. Confusion arises because gold is traded like a commodity, yet gold is not a commodity, it is money."

JAMES G. RICKARDS

(James G. Rickards is the author of The Road to Ruin: The Global Elites' Secret Plan for the Next Financial Crisis. James G. Rickards is an American lawyer, economist, investment banker, speaker, media commentator, and author on matters of finance and precious metals. He graduated from Johns Hopkins University in 1973 with a Bachelor of Arts degree with honors, and in 1974, from the Paul H. Nitze School of Advanced International Studies in Washington, D.C., with an M.A. in international economics. He received his Juris Doctor from the University of Pennsylvania Law School and a Master of Laws in taxation from New York University School of Law. He has held senior positions at Citibank, Long-Term Capital Management, and Caxton Associates. Rickards worked on Wall Street for 35 years.)

How Does Gold Relate to Money?

- For the vast majority of the 20th century, the United States dollar's value was connected and tied directly to gold. As a brief history lesson, after World War II ended, the "Bretton Woods" system was created, which attached the U.S. dollar to gold and the world's other major currencies (money) to the United States dollar. The "Bretton Woods" agreement made the United States dollar the world's reserve currency.

- The United States dollar was backed by Gold until August 15, 1971.

- In 1971, under the direction of President Richard Nixon, the United States and the Federal government decided to no longer back U.S. currency by gold, thus severing the dollar's connection to the price of gold. If I were somebody who was into highlighting or taking notes I would get out a highlighter and I would highlight the statement below.

- By deciding to no longer back the U.S. dollar with gold, President Richard Nixon basically created a scenario where the United States government could produce unlimited amounts of dollars when needed, which has caused and created a situation where the value of every U.S. dollar in circulation declines in value every year. The more money that the government prints, the less each dollar in circulation is worth. This phenomenon of devaluing currency as a result of exponentially creating more and more money that is not backed by anything is called inflation.

NOTABLE QUOTABLE

"Inflation is as violent as a mugger, as frightening
as an armed robber and as deadly as a hit man."

PRESIDENT RONALD WILSON REAGAN

*(Ronald Wilson Reagan (February 6, 1911 – June 5, 2004) was an
American politician and actor who served as the 40th president of the
United States from 1981 to 1989. As a member of the Republican Party, he
became an important figure in the American conservative movement.
The period encompassing his presidency is known as the Reagan era.)*

Why Is the Bretton Woods Agreement Called "The Bretton Woods" Agreement?

"The Bretton Woods Agreement" is referred to as "The Bretton Woods Agreement" because it was created at the official United Nations Monetary and Financial Conference which was held in July of 1944 in a small town by the name of Bretton Woods, New Hampshire. This conference which changed the course of financial history for America and the rest of the world was held at the Mount Washington Hotel. At this meeting delegates from a total of 44 nations sat down and agreed on the creation and layout of the new post-World War II economic system.

"The Bretton Woods Agreement" created the framework for countries to interact with each other monetarily and it resulted in the creation of the International Monetary Fund (IMF) and the International Bank for Reconstruction and Development (World Bank). The Bretton Woods Agreement established an international

23

monetary system which featured fixed exchange rates that were connected to and "pegged" to the U.S. dollar, with the U.S. dollar being convertible to gold which would be set at a price of $35 per ounce. "The Bretton Woods Agreement" created global economic stability while placing the United States of America as the leader and the head of this newly agreed upon international monetary system. This international monetary system was anchored on the idea that the U.S. dollar would be the world's reserve currency and that the U.S. dollar would be backed by gold.

I would highly recommend that you take a moment to mentally marinate on the harsh reality and the power-packed profundity of the idea that "The Bretton Woods Agreement" collapsed in 1971 when President Richard Nixon decided to end the U.S. dollar-gold convertibility. Since 1971, the United States of America has been allowed to print money without limit while racking up a mind-blowing amount of debt. Just to provide a little context for how much debt the United States of America has now accumulated I would encourage you consider the following facts:

1. As of February of 2026, the United States of America is nearly $39 trillion in debt.

2. As of February of 2026, the national debt comes out to roughly $357,068 per United States tax payer.

3. As of February of 2026, America's national debt is much larger than the size of our entire GDP. What is GDP? Gross domestic product (GDP) means the sum of all goods and services produced by the U.S. economy.

4. As of February of 2026, Japan is the biggest foreign holder of United States debt? As of May 2025, Japan was holding more than $1.1 trillion, or 3.1%, of America's total debt.

5. Historically, both Democratic and Republican lead administrations have chosen to spend money that they did not have by simply choosing to print more and more money, which causes the value of the U.S. dollar to go down, down and down.

What Were the Keypoints of the Bretton Woods Agreement?

- Under the Bretton Woods Agreement, the United States dollar became cemented as the world's dominant global reserve currency and transaction currency, a status that the United States maintains and enjoys today.

- Under the Bretton Woods Agreement, the member countries agreed to peg their currencies to the United States dollar at fixed rates.

- The Bretton Woods Agreement introduced the Gold-Dollar Standard. The United States dollar was connected (backed by) to gold ($35 per ounce). This agreement made the United States dollar effectively the world's global standard.

- The creation of the International Monetary Fund (IMF): The International Monetary Fund was created to monitor the exchange rates and to provide short-term loans to countries around the world with balance-of-payments issues.

- The International Bank for Reconstruction and Development (IBRD): The International Bank for Reconstruction and Development was the precursor to the creation of the World Bank, which was focused on post-war reconstruction and development.

How Did the Bretton Woods Agreement Collapse?

- The Bretton Woods agreement began to be strained as a result of massive U.S. military spending and the colossal overall deficits generated by the Federal Government of the United States which lead to excess dollars being printed and being used abroad.

- In 1971, President Richard Nixon chose to end the U.S. dollar's convertibility to gold (closing the "gold window"), effectively ending the fixed-rate system. Again, there is no proof that President Richard Nixon was or wasn't drunk when he decided to end the U.S. dollar's convertibility to gold (closing the "gold window"), effectively ending the fixed-rate system. What was President Nixon thinking? Was President Nixon thinking?

What Does It Mean for America to Be the World's Reserve Currency?

- The United States dollar has been, and still is (as of 2026), the world's primary reserve currency; and this is UNBELIEVABLY IMPORTANT. The United States dollar is held by central banks, which they use for trade, debt, and stability, with a roughly 58% share of global foreign exchange reserves as of mid-2025. If the United States were to ever lose its status as the "World's Reserve Currency" the standard of living for every American would collapse immediately!

- Over time the United States has been slowly using its dominance as the "World's Reserve Currency."

- Although only foreign governments and central banks were allowed to redeem (exchange) dollars for gold, this linking of the U.S. dollar to gold (that ended in 1971) created confidence in the monetary system and created a sustainable and stable relationship between the United States, the dollar, and the global economy.

- When President Richard Nixon decided to de-link the United States Dollar from gold in 1971, this ended the dollar-for-gold convertibility and the dollar's status as being "gold-backed." Thus, from this point forward, the United States dollar has been a fiat currency, which is only backed by the confidence and trust of the American people, the confidence and trust that other countries have about the United States of America, and its ability to pay money to the institutions and countries it owes money to.

FUN FACTS:

1971 | What the Hell Happened to the World in 1971?

» Why Did the Following Events All Take Place In 1971? The World Economic Forum Began, Nixon Took U.S. Off the Gold Standard, U.S. Began Legalizing Abortions, Rules for Radicals Was Written & Dedicated to Lucifer, the Pope Builds Snake Head Shaped Building (See Citations)

1971 | Why Was Rules for Radicals (Which Is Dedicated to Lucifer) Which Is Often Quoted by Barack Obama and Hillary Clinton Written by Saul Alinsky Written In 1971? - Learn More - https://thehill.com/blogs/ballot-box/presidential-races/288457-carson-explains-lucifer-comment-clinton-and-alinksy-on-a/

1971 | Why Did America Begin Legalizing Abortions (Sacrificing Babies to BAAL) In 1971?

» Remembering an Era Before Roe, When New York Had the 'Most Liberal' Abortion Law - Learn More - https://www.nytimes.com/2018/07/19/us/politics/new-york-abortion-roe-wade-nyt.html

» **When Abortion Was Only Legal In 6 States** - Learn More - https://fivethirtyeight.com/features/when-abortion-was-only-legal-in-6-states/

1971 | Why Was America Taken Off of the Gold Standard by President Richard Nixon Per the Recommendation of Henry Kissinger In 1971?

» The United States under the leadership of President Richard Nixon in 1971, ended the dollar convertibility to gold and implemented wage and price controls, which soon brought an end to the Bretton Woods System. - READ - https://www.federalreservehistory.org/essays/gold-convertibility-ends

» Henry Alfred Kissinger served as the Secretary of State under President Richard M. Nixon.

1971 | Why Did Klaus Schwab Found the World Economic Forum In 1971 Per the Recommendation of Henry Kissinger? https://www.weforum.org/agenda/2019/12/world-economic-forum-davos-at-50-history-a-timeline-of-highlights/

> » Video Clip #1 - https://www.youtube.com/watch?v=ApPQlu3RvLU
>
> » Video Clip #2 - https://www.youtube.com/watch?v=HTmzbSFNK2c
>
> » Video Clip #3 - https://www.youtube.com/watch?v=7_Xw5tWsOQo
>
> » Henry Kissinger made a big impression on Klaus Schwab - https://www.youtube.com/watch?v=HTmzbSFNK2c

1971 | Why Did the Pope Complete The Paul VI Audience Hall In the Shape of a Snake Head In 1971? (Italian: Aula Paolo VI) also known as the Hall of the Pontifical Audiences is a building in Rome named for Pope Paul VI with a seating capacity of 6,300, designed in reinforced concrete by the Italian architect Pier Luigi Nervi and completed in 1971. [1] It was constructed on land donated by the Knights of Columbus.

> » https://hope-of-israel.org/popeshall.html
>
> » A look inside "Snake Head Building" - https://www.youtube.com/watch?v=ushhDUM3Hos

1971 | Why Was The Darkseid / New Gods Comic Book Series Which Prophesied the "The Fourth World" / The Fourth Industrial Revolution Written In 1971? - READ - https://en.wikipedia.org/wiki/Darkseid

1971 | Why Was Disney World Featuring the Experimental Prototype Community of Tomorrow (EPCOT Center) Opened to the Public On October 1st 1971? - READ - https://en.wikipedia.org/wiki/Epcot

1971 | Why Did John Lennon Write & Record "Imagine" Prophesying Klaus Schwab's "Great Reset" Vision?

"You'll own nothing and you'll be happy" (alternatively "You'll own nothing and be happy") is a phrase that was famously published by the World Economic Forum (WEF) based on a 2016 essay written by Danish politician Ida Auken about a dystopian vision for the future in which humans live in and rely on a sharing-based economy for many of their needs.

John Lennon wrote the song "Imagine" for the 1971 album by the same name. The song "Imagine" was the best-selling single of his solo career, the lyrics encourage listeners to think about a communist world filled with "world of peace" and a future that is filled with a world without religion and its concepts, without economic materialism, and without borders separating nations. Shortly before John Lennon's death, Lennon said that most of the song's lyrics and content came from the mind of his wife, Yoko Ono, and in 2017, she received a co-writing credit.

The "Imagine" lyrics written by John Lennon and Yoko Ono
are written below:

Imagine there's no heaven

It's easy if you try

No hell below us

Above us only sky

Imagine all the people

Living for today, ah

Imagine there's no countries

It isn't hard to do

Nothing to kill or die for

And no religion too

Imagine all the people

Living life in peace, you

You may say I'm a dreamer

But I'm not the only one

I hope someday you'll join us

And the world will be as one

Imagine no possessions

I wonder if you can

No need for greed or hunger

A brotherhood of man

Imagine all the people

Sharing all the world, you

You may say I'm a dreamer

But I'm not the only one

I hope someday you'll join us

And the world will live as one

NOTABLE QUOTABLE

"In the absence of the gold standard, there is no way to protect savings from confiscation through inflation. There is no safe store of value."

ALAN GREENSPAN

(Alan Greenspan is an American economist who served as the 13th chairman of the Federal Reserve from 1987 to 2006. He worked as a private adviser and provided consulting for firms through his company, Greenspan Associates LLC. First nominated to the Federal Reserve by President Ronald Reagan in August 1987, Greenspan was reappointed at successive four-year intervals until retiring on January 31, 2006, after the second-longest tenure in the position, behind only William McChesney Martin.)

FUN FACTS:

» When measuring gold there is a difference between the world "tons" and the word "tonnes." Tonnes (metric) and tons (US short) are actually different weights. A tonne (t) is 1,000 kg (approx. 2,204.6 lbs), while a ton (short ton) is 2,000 lbs (approx. 907.18 kg). Thus, a "tonne" is much heavier and this is the correct term to use when discussing precious metals in large quantities, often referring to metric tonnes. When discussing gold, a metric tonne equals about 32,150.7 troy ounces, which makes it a much larger and more valuable quantity than a US short ton.

» "YUGE" is a term used by President Donald J. Trump to reference large things. As an example, one could say, "America has a YUGE amount of national debt."

What Happens If America Were to Lose Its Status As the World's Reserve Currency?

- If America were to lose its status as the World's Reserve Currency, many experts believe that the financial situation for the average American would become worse than the great depression.

- As of 2026, the BRICS alliance (Brazil, Russia, India, China, South Africa) are actively developing a gold-backed, digital reserve currency and settlement unit which is being referred to as the "Unit" or "BRICS Pay." The purpose of this plan is to reduce the world's dependence on the U.S. Dollar as the World's Reserve Currency for trade, which would GREATLY mitigate (reduce) the impact and risks associated with sanctions imposed by America and America's international power.

- The BRICS nations are focused and committed to the process of "de-dollarization"; thus, day by day and year by year, the BRICS nations have been consistently buying up the world's gold supply. Daily, the BRICS nations are openly accumulating the earth's gold reserves with the stated goal of shifting away from dollar reliance, with Russia now holding 2,336 tonnes of gold, China holding 2,298 tonnes of gold and India now holding 880 tonnes of gold as of 2025.

- The BRICS alliance is now reported to control approximately 50% of all global gold production which is signalling the BRICS alliance's increased economic leverage and ability to challenge U.S. dollar dominance.

- During February of 2022, the Western nations chose to freeze over 300 billion dollars of Russia's central bank reserves. Thus as of February 2022, the largest financial seizure in modern history took place and demonstrated the dangers of currency vulnerability and countries like Russia being connected to the U.S. dollar. The freezing (taking or stealing) of Russia's $300 billion was the single event that is often credited for being the final prompt needed by the BRICS countries to recognize that it was now time for many of the earth's nations to dramatically reduce their connection to the U.S. Dollar. As a result, Russia focused on gold accumulation and reached 75 million ounces worth and 229 billion dollars of gold accumulation as of April 2025, which helped them to offset frozen assets.

- In order to prepare to introduce the new gold-backed BRICS currency, the BRICS nations have been hoarding (buying copious amounts of) gold. The BRICS are now reported to have accumulated more than 50% of the global gold supply.

- As of 2026 the BRICS alliance has full member countries, and has successfully expanded beyond its original five members. The BRICS alliance includes the following 11 full member countries:
  - Brazil
  - Russia
  - India
  - China
  - South Africa
  - Egypt
  - Ethiopia
  - Iran
  - Saudi Arabia
  - United Arab Emiraterates (UAE)
  - Indonesia

- The BRICS countries now represent roughly 40% of the earth's human population and 37% of global gross domestic product. - Learn More About BRICS - https://www.weforum.org/stories/2024/11/brics-summit-geopolitics-bloc-international/

BRICS FUN FACTS:

» The term "BRIC" was originally created by British economist Jim O'Neill. The term "BRIC" was then consistently used by his employer, Goldman Sachs 2021 to refer to a group of emerging markets.

» In 2009, the BRIC" bloc hosted their inaugural summit featuring: Brazil, Russia, India, and China.

» In 2010, South Africa joined the "BRIC" bloc in September of 2010. The group was then renamed to be BRICS.

» Since 2024, the acronym BRICS+ or BRICS Plus has been used to reference the new membership that has joined the BLOC, however we believe the group might want to consider using the acronym of: BRICSEEISUAEI to be easier for people to remember...

» The BRICS+ block has successfully implemented many initiatives with the aim of completely reforming the global financial system, such as the creation of the New Development Bank. The bank is headquartered in Shanghai, China (which is a country that most believe to be the biggest threat to the United States both financially and militarily). The first regional office for the New Development bank was opened in Johannesburg, South Africa in 2016.

» At the 2015 BRICS summit which was hosted in Russia, ministers from the BRICS states decided to move forward with the creation of a payment system that would be an alternative to the SWIFT system. The official stated goal of BRICS pay was to initially move to settlements in national currencies.

» What is SWIFT? The Society for Worldwide Interbank Financial Telecommunication (SWIFT), legally S.W.I.F.T. SC, is a cooperative established in 1973 in Belgium (French: Société Coopérative) and owned by the banks and other member firms that use its service.

What Happens If the SWIFT System Ever Stop Being Used?

• Many respected financial experts believe that a shift away from the SWIFT (Society for Worldwide Interbank Financial Telecommunication) messaging system, would trigger a massive restructuring of the global financial system which currently acknowledges the U.S. dollar as the world's reserve currency. Many experts believe that if the U.S. dollar (USD) ever stopped being used by the majority of the world as the primary global reserve currency, this would trigger a process often called "de-dollarization" which would lead to the dramatic collapse of the standard of living of every American.

What Does the Concept "World's Reserve Currency" Mean?

- A reserve currency is a foreign currency that is held by governments, central banks or other monetary authorities as part of their foreign exchange reserve. The reserve currency can then be used in international transactions, international investments and all aspects of the global economy. The world's "reserve currency" is often considered a hard currency or safe-haven currency. The U.S. Dollar (USD) remains the world's dominant reserve currency, accounting for approximately 57% of global foreign exchange reserves as of Q3 2025.

"What does the debt of \$33 trillion tell us about? It is about the emission. Nevertheless, it is the main weapon used by the United States to preserve its power across the world. As soon as the political leadership decided to use the US dollar as a tool of political struggle, a blow was dealt to this American power. I would not like to use any strong language, but it is a stupid thing to do and a grave mistake. Look at what is going on in the world. Even the United States allies are now downsizing their dollar reserves...Do you even realize what is going on or not? Does anyone in the United States realize this? What are you doing? You're cutting yourself off. All experts say this. Ask any intelligent and thinking person in the United States what the dollar means for the US. You're killing it with your own hands."

- VLADIMIR PUTIN (PRESIDENT OF RUSSIA), AS OF FEBRUARY 8TH 2024

("The Vladimir Putin Interview" is a television interview hosted by the American journalist and political commentator Tucker Carlson with the Russian president Vladimir Putin. It premiered on the Tucker Carlson Network and the social media website Twitter on February 8, 2024.)

NOTABLE QUOTABLE

"Economic medicine that was previously meted out by the cupful has recently been dispensed by the barrel. These once unthinkable dosages will almost certainly bring on unwelcome after-effects. Their precise nature is anyone's guess, though one likely consequence is an onslaught of inflation."

WARREN BUFFETT

(Warren Edward Buffett is an American investor and philanthropist who is the chairman and former CEO of the conglomerate Berkshire Hathaway. As a result of his success, Buffett is one of the best-known investors in America. According to Forbes, as of January 2026, Buffett's estimated net worth stood at US$148.9 billion, making him the ninth-richest individual in the world. Buffett was born in Omaha, Nebraska. The son of U.S. congressman and businessman Howard Buffett, he developed an interest in business and investing during his youth. He entered the Wharton School of the University of Pennsylvania in 1947, before graduating from the University of Nebraska in Lincoln. He went on to graduate from Columbia Business School where he molded his investment philosophy around the concept of value investing pioneered by Benjamin Graham.)

Is the BRICS (Brazil, Russian, India, China & South Africa) Alliance Developing a Common Currency to Rival the U.S. Dollar And to Replace the U.S. Dollar As the World's Reserve Currency of Choice?

BREAKING NEWS!!! This just in...At the BRICS 2025 summit in Johannesburg, the BRICS alliance member states announced what many economists had speculated. The BRICS alliance bloc is openly developing, testing, and prototyping a gold-backed digital settlement system which will be possibly tied to a basket of commodities including: gold, oil, strategic minerals, and a weighted index of national currencies.

The BRICS alliance has openly and publicly began simulations using blockchain (programmable money) smart contracts which can be used for automated settlements and reserve banking for price stability.

Although (as of February 2026) the BRICS digital currency has not yet been deployed, it has been designed to serve as a neutral intermediary for cross-border transactions, which would be able to bypass the U.S. dollar's gatekeeping role and to forever limit the Western leverage over the earth's global financial system.

What Is Inflation?

Inflation is what happens to the value of your dollars when your government chooses to spend money they do not have on things they cannot afford. As your government continues to print more and more money that is not backed by anything other than the faith and confidence of its citizens, the spending power of the money gradually decreases while the confidence of the citizens gradually decreases in their government that is printing all the money.

In general and over a period of time, inflation can be experienced as a sustained increase in the prices of every good and service that they buy. Inflation decreases the value of the hard-earned money that you have without your consent. Eventually, as the cost of living goes up and up and the currency being issued has less and less purchasing power, hyper-inflation becomes a harsh reality as the currency eventually becomes worth nothing. Inflation is commonly measured by what is known as the Consumer Price Index (CPI). Inflation simply means that the purchasing power of your hard-earned money is going down in value every day while the cost of everything is going up, up and up.

Throughout the history of the planet, nearly every leader, president, mayor, governor, king or prime Minister has found it impossible to successfully serve his two constituencies without using inflation. Taxpayers are perpetually angry about what taxes they have to pay (and they never want to pay more), while those receiving government support want more government support and funding to pay for the causes that they perceive to be needed (including pension, military spending, roads, healthcare, free college and more).

Thus, with the goal of making everybody happy, nearly all leaders choose to simply print money they don't have to give people things that the government cannot afford to give them without raising taxes on the taxpayers who are already upset about how much money they are paying in taxes. Thus as a result, almost historically without exception, every country experiences a gradual decline, and ultimately exponential decline, in the value of their national currency, which is what we call "inflation."

NOTABLE QUOTABLE

"Inflation is the greatest enemy of all the people and of our hopes for economic growth. It is at the bottom of the problems that we're trying to solve."

PRESIDENT RONALD WILSON REAGAN

(Ronald Wilson Reagan (February 6, 1911 – June 5, 2004) was an American politician and actor who served as the 40th president of the United States from 1981 to 1989. A member of the Republican Party, he became an important figure in the American conservative movement. The period encompassing his presidency is known as the Reagan era.)

Can Inflation Be Stopped?

- No.

- As of the time that this book is being written (January of 2026), the United States is officially $39 trillion in debt, which is over $357,068 sof debt per United States citizen.

- The interest payments alone on the national debt have become a mind-boggling expense of over $1 trillion annually, which means that the annual interest payments that the United States government is making on our national debt exceed our spending on national defense.

- Attempting to get the United States government to balance the budget is a lot like bringing your decapitated dog to your local veterinarian and asking him if he can help to save your family dog.

- The total amount of debt that the United States government claims to have doesn't even factor in the "unfunded liabilities" of Social Security and Medicare which are estimated to be $78.3 trillion over 75 years by some analyses.

NOTABLE QUOTABLE

"In the simplest terms, inflation occurs when there's too much money in the system. On the flip side, deflation occurs when there are too few dollars in circulation."

ROBERT KIYOSAKI

(Robert Kiyosaki is an international best-selling author of the Rich Dad Poor Dad book series, a legendary real estate investor, multiple-time ThrivetimeShow.com podcast guest, and entrepreneur. Kiyosaki is the author of more than 26 books, including the international self-published personal finance Rich Dad Poor Dad series of books which has been translated into 51 languages and sold over 41 million copies worldwide.)

If Inflation Can't Be Stopped, Have Currencies Ever Collapsed COMPLETELY?

Yes. In fact, listed below you will find a brief overview of the history of modern inflation. The most recent example of hyperinflation can be found in Venezuela, after the Communists took over this once free and prosperous country.

- **France, May 1795**

  - Highest monthly inflation: 150%
  - Prices doubled every 15 days.

- **Germany, October 1923**

  - Highest monthly inflation: 29,500%
  - Prices doubled every 3.7 days

- **Greece, October 1944**

  - Highest monthly inflation: 13,800%
  - Prices doubled every 4.3 days

- **Hungary, August 1945**

  - Prices doubled every 15 hours

- **China, October 1947**

  - Prices doubled every 5.3 days.
  - Read the Full Story: After World War Two, China was divided by civil war. Nationalists and Communists battled for control of the country and introduced competing currencies in the process, leaving China's monetary system fragmented among ten major mediums of exchange in 1948.

- Currency took center stage at times during the conflict – Campbell and Tullock (1954) explained that the three governments (including the Japanese occupiers) engaged in "monetary warfare" by attempting to undermine opposing currencies in various ways.

- To fund the conflict, the Nationalists resorted to running huge budget deficits, which they eventually looked to cover by printing money, leading to runaway hyperinflation. (This was preceded by the abandonment of the silver standard in China in 1935). They even got the Taiwanese central bank involved with the monetization scheme, which caused hyperinflation in Taiwan as well. Learn More At: https://www.businessinsider.com/worst-hyperinflation-episodes-in-history-2013-9#yugoslaviarepublika-srpska-april-1992-january-1994-3

• Nicaragua, June 1986

- Highest monthly inflation: 120%

- Prices doubled every 16 days

• Peru, July 1990

- Highest monthly inflation: 150%

- Prices doubled every 13 days

- Read the Full Story: Peru had a long battle with inflation in the latter half of the 20th century. During the first half of the 1980s, Fernando Belaunde Terry was president, and Peru was faced with austerity policies imposed by IMF lenders following the Latin American financial crisis that began early in the decade.

- ◦ Economist Thayer Watkins says the Belaunde Terry administration gave the appearance that it was complying with the reforms recommended by the IMF, when in reality, it was not. The economy was suffering stagflation at the time, and it was blamed on IMF austerity policies by the electorate, even though those policies weren't actually being followed.

- ◦ This led to the election of Alan Garcia in 1985 as president. Garcia enacted populist economic reforms that only served to weaken the economy and shut Peru out of international credit markets. Faced with a lack of access to credit and deteriorating economic conditions, sustained high inflation became hyperinflation in Peru. Learn More At: https://www.businessinsider.com/worst-hyperinflation-episodes-in-history-2013-9#yugoslaviarepublika-srpska-april-1992-january-1994-3

- **Yugoslavia, January 1994**

  - ◦ Highest monthly inflation: 313,000,000%

  - ◦ Prices doubled every 1.4 days

  - ◦ Read the Full Story: The fall of the Soviet Union led to a decreased international role for Yugoslavia – formerly a key geopolitical player connecting East and West – and its ruling Communist party eventually came under the same pressure as the Soviets did. This led to a breakup of Yugoslavia into several countries along ethnic lines and subsequent wars over the following years as the newly-formed political entities sorted out their independence.

- In the process, trade among the regions of the former Yugoslavia collapsed, and industrial output followed. At the same time, an international embargo was placed on Yugoslavian exports, which further crushed output.

- Petrovic, Bogetic, and Vujosevic (1998) explain that the newly-formed Federal Republic of Yugoslavia, in contrast with other states that broke away like Serbia and Croatia, retained much of the bloated bureaucracy that existed before the split, contributing to the federal deficit. In an attempt to monetize this and other deficits, the central bank lost control of money creation and caused hyperinflation. Learn more today at: https://www.businessinsider.com/worst-hyperinflation-episodes-in-history-2013-9#yugoslaviarepublika-srpska-april-1992-january-1994-3

• Zimbabwe, November 2008

- Highest monthly inflation: 79,600,000,000%

- Prices doubled every 24.7 hours

- Read the Full Story: Zimbabwe's hyperinflation was preceded by a long, grinding decline in economic output that followed Robert Mugabe's land reforms of 2000-2001, through which land was expropriated largely from white farmers and redistributed to the majority black populace. This led to a 50 percent collapse in output over the next nine years.

- Socialist reforms and a costly involvement in Congo's civil war led to outsized government budget deficits. At the same time, the Zimbabwean population was declining as people fled the country.

These two opposing factors of increased government spending and a decreasing tax base caused the government to resort to monetization of its fiscal deficit. Learn More At: https://www.businessinsider.com/worst-hyperinflation-episodes-in-history-2013-9#yugoslaviarepublika-srpska-april-1992-january-1994-3

- **Venezuela, 2013**

  ○ Prices rose 41% in 2013
  ○ 2018 inflation was 65,000%.

If Inflation Can't Be Stopped, What Can You Do to Protect Your Wealth?

- Buy silver and gold and hold.

- Buy real estate and wait.

NOTABLE QUOTABLE

"You cannot control what happens to you, but you
can control your attitude toward what happens
to you, and in that, you will be mastering change
rather than allowing it to master you."

BRIAN TRACY

*(Brian Tracy is a Canadian-American motivational public speaker and
self-development author. He is the author of over eighty books that have
been translated into dozens of languages. His popular books are Earn
What You're Really Worth, Eat That Frog!, No Excuses! The Power of
Self-Discipline, and The Psychology of Achievement.)*

How Much Has the Price of Gold Increased Since the United States Moved Off of the Gold Standard In 1971?

- **1971** – In 1971, the price of an ounce of gold was officially set at **$35 per ounce** until President Richard Nixon took the United States off of the gold standard.

- **1985** – Gold averaged a price of **approximately $332.85 per ounce** in 1985.

- **1995** – Gold averaged a price of **approximately $384 per ounce** in 1995.

- **2005** – Gold averaged a price of **approximately $445 per ounce** in 2005.

- **2015** – Gold averaged a price of **approximately $1,160 per ounce** in 2015.

- **2025** – Gold averaged a price of **approximately $3,435 per ounce** in 2025

- **2026** – Gold is priced at **approximately $5,169 per ounce** in 2026 (as this book is being written).

If you sit down and compare the spot price of gold against the spot price in the year 1999 to the value of gold in 2026, the value of gold has gone from $279 per ounce to $4,919.60 per ounce. This means that gold has gone up in value by over ten times since 1995 alone! Thus, unless you were an early investor in Tesla, Amazon, Apple, or IBM, it is very unlikely that you would have been able to create such a return on investment as you would have gotten through the purchasing of gold and silver. And as the world gets more and more wild, silver and gold are (and remain as) assets that have monetary value and industrial value. Thus, they actually thrive and do exceedingly well when the world is filled with fear and anxiety about the future, whereas many stocks fall and bottom out when people have concerns about the world economy or the United States economy.

NOTABLE QUOTABLE

"Gold and silver coins will protect from the coming financial crash"

JAMES G. RICKARDS

(James G. Rickards is the author of The Road to Ruin: The Global Elites' Secret Plan for the Next Financial Crisis. James G. Rickards is an American lawyer, economist, investment banker, speaker, media commentator, and author on matters of finance and precious metals. He graduated from Johns Hopkins University in 1973 with a Bachelor of Arts degree with honors, and in 1974, from the Paul H. Nitze School of Advanced International Studies in Washington, D.C., with an M.A. in international economics. He received his Juris Doctor from the University of Pennsylvania Law School and a Master of Laws in taxation from New York University School of Law. He has held senior positions at Citibank, Long-Term Capital Management, and Caxton Associates. Rickards worked on Wall Street for 35 years.)

Was President Richard Nixon Drunk When He Decided to Take the U.S. Dollar Off of the Gold Standard In 1971?

- We have no proof that President Richard Nixon was or wasn't drunk when he decided to take the U.S. dollar off of the gold standard in 1971.

NOTABLE QUOTABLE

"You have to choose between trusting to the natural stability of gold and the natural stability of the honesty and intelligence of the members of the Government. And, with due respect for these gentlemen, I advise you, as long as the capitalist system lasts, to vote for gold."

GEORGE BERNARD SHAW

(George Bernard Shaw, known at his insistence as Bernard Shaw, was an Irish playwright, critic, polemicist and political activist. His influence on Western theatre, culture and politics extended from the 1880s to his death and beyond.)

What Are Petrodollars And How Do They Relate to the Value of the U.S. Dollar?

The term "petrodollar" is in reference to United States dollars that are earned from selling crude oil exports. The petrodollar system was a 50-year agreement and deal that ended in June of 2024. In summary, the petrodollar was an agreement that Saudi Arabia had to price and sell oil using United States dollars. Those dollars were then to be used to buy US Treasuries. The 50-year petrodollar agreement between Saudi Arabia and the United States ended on June 9th of 2024. The agreement was allowed to expire, with the country of Saudi Arabia deciding not to renew the 50-year agreement. Petrodollars played an integral part in the global economy we now live in. The concept of petrodollars began to show up in the early 1970s after President Richard Nixon chose to no longer back the U.S. dollar by gold.

In the early 70s and still today (as of 2026) oil sales and surpluses are measured using U.S. dollars because the U.S. dollar is the world's reserve currency of choice and because the United States is still hanging on to our status as the world's largest economy.

Although the average person does not talk about or think about it, the petrodollar system has quietly been the backbone of the U.S. dollar's perceived value around the world since the 1970s. Since the time of the Cold War between the United States and the Soviet Union, countries that export oil (especially Saudi Arabia and other OPEC, The Organization of the Petroleum Exporting Countries, members) agreed to price crude oil exclusively in United States dollars in exchange for perpetual protection from the United States military, arms sales and other strategic partnerships.

This agreement created a perpetual demand for the U.S. dollars that were no longer backed by gold. The global demand for oil created an endless demand for non-gold-backed U.S. dollars, which then created more demand for the U.S. Treasury securities. Around the world, the non-gold-backed U.S. dollar became recognized as a relevant medium of exchange, and it by default became the world's default reserve currency. Does this make sense?

The petrodollar is what allowed the non-gold backed U.S. fiat currency (U.S. dollar) to have value around the world despite the fact that the U.S. dollar can now be printed infinitely and it is not backed by anything other the trust and confidence that people around the world have in the actual fiat currency. Imagine that you and your family were allowed to infinitely print money! Think about that? Imagine that you could infinitely operate your family budget at a massive deficit because you were the only family in your state that was allowed to infinitely create your own supply of money. How do you believe that the other citizens living in your state would feel once they discovered that you were able to live large and be in charge because you were the only family who had access to an infinite "magic money printing machine."

However, since 2025, that era of the petrodollar has been fraying and has been coming apart quickly. The cracks in the petrodollar system are no longer just theoretical, ideological or potential. The cracks in the petrodollar system are factual, provable, structural, urgent, institutional, obvious and geopolitical.

In case you missed it, or in case I did a poor job of explaining this earlier, YOU AND I NEED TO BE AWARE OF THE FACT THAT, The BRICS alliance countries (Brazil, Russia, India, China & South Africa) are now openly, and actively creating a financial system that will free them from their reliance upon the U.S. dollar and it is going to be gold-backed.

The decline of the petrodollar is now aggressively and openly being stimulated for a variety of converging reasons including:

- The world is tired of watching the world's largest debtor nation (The United States) have access to an unlimited "magic money system" that allows us (the United States) to print infinite amounts of money.

- The world is tired of watching the EPIC U.S. fiscal dysfunction, which is a constant reminder that the world is trusting the U.S. dollar's value less and less every day.

- The BRICS alliance (Brazil, Russia, India, China & South Africa) have been buying up the world's gold supply in preparation to introduce a new gold-backed currency to rival the United States dollar as the world's reserve currency of choice.

NOTABLE QUOTABLE

"Commodities such as gold and silver have a world market that transcends national borders, politics, religions, and race. A person may not like someone else's religion, but he'll accept his gold."

ROBERT KIYOSAKI

(Robert Kiyosaki is an international best-selling author of the Rich Dad Poor Dad book series, a legendary real estate investor, multiple-time ThrivetimeShow.com podcast guest, and entrepreneur. Kiyosaki is the author of more than 26 books, including the international self-published personal finance Rich Dad Poor Dad series of books which has been translated into 51 languages and sold over 41 million copies worldwide.)

The Dollar is Losing Credibility: why central banks are scrambling for gold

Experts say central banks are increasingly stuffing their vaults as an insurance policy in a volatile world –

A growing number of central banks to hastily amass vast stockpiles of gold, upending decades of conventional economic logic and fuelling an increase in the gold price amid mounting geopolitical tensions (Richard Partington, "The Dollar Is Losing Credibility: Why Central Banks Are Scrambling For Gold," TheGuardian.com, Jan. 16, 2026, https://www.theguardian.com/business/2026/jan/16/the-dollar-is-losing-credibility-why-central-banks-are-scrambling-for-gold).

China's Secretive Gold Purchases Help Fuel Record Rally -

"CHINA'S unreported gold purchases could be more than 10 times its official figures, as the country quietly tries to diversify away from the US dollar, say analysts, highlighting the increasingly opaque sources of demand behind bullion's record-breaking rally.

Publicly reported buying by China's central bank has been so low this year – 1.9 tonnes purchased in August, 1.9 tonnes in July and 2.2 tonnes in June – that few in the market believe the official figures.

"China is buying gold as part of their de-dollarisation strategy," said Jeff Currie, chief strategy officer of energy pathways at Carlyle, adding that he does not try to guess how much gold the People's Bank of China (PBOC) is buying.

"Unlike oil, where you can track it with satellites, with gold you can't. There's just no way to know where this stuff goes and who is buying it." Central banks have been buying up huge quantities of bullion in recent years, fuelling a rally that has pushed the price above US$4,300 per troy ounce. World Gold Council (WGC) data shows that over the past decade, gold's share of global reserves outside the US has climbed from 10 to 26 per cent, making it the second-largest reserve asset after the US dollar" (Leslie Hook, "China's Secretive Gold Purchases Help Fuel Record Rally," BusinessTimes.com, https://www.businesstimes.com.sg/international/global/chinas-secretive-gold-purchases-help-fuel-record-rally).

Stockpiling Gold

Countries with the largest gold reserves in the world
in the second quarter of 2025 (in metric tons)

**5-year trend
(since Q2 2020)**

Country	Reserves	5-year trend
United States	8,133	0
Germany	3,350	-13
Italy	2,452	0
France	2,437	+1
Russia	2,330*	+30
China	2,299	+351
Switzerland	1,040*	0
India	880	+219
Japan	846	+81

* Russia and Switzerland: data from the first quarter of 2025 (latest available)
Source: World Gold Council

statista

The Statista graph above depicts the countries with the largest gold
reserves as of Q2 2025) To see the graph in full or learn more, visit:
https://www.statista.com/chart/19123/countries-with-the-largest-gold-
reserves-and-change-over-the-last-years/

Breaking: The FT Confirms China's Secretive Gold Buying

As noted in this space prior breaking down reports from Goldman Sachs, Soc Gen, and others over the last three years; the following can be restated: China's central bank and related entities appear to be buying far more gold (up to 10x more) than they officially report, creating a large and opaque source of demand that is closely tied to a broader effort to reduce exposure to the US dollar and that helps explain the current record bullion prices (Vince Lanci, "Breaking: The FT Confirms China's Secretive Gold Buying," JPost.com, https://www.jpost.com/business-and-innovation/precious-metals/article-874231).

China's secretive gold purchases help fuel record rally

- https://www.ft.com/content/b77a95b0-ee74-4bde-b11f-32ee0fe03cd8

China's central bank buys gold for 15th consecutive month

"China's central bank extended its gold buying spree for a 15th month in January, data from the People's Bank of China (PBOC) showed on Saturday.

The country's gold holdings rose to 74.19 million fine troy ounces by the end of January, up from 74.15 million the previous month" (Reuters, "China's Central Bank Buys Gold For 15th Consecutive Month," Reuters.com, Feb. 6, 2026, https://www.reuters.com/world/china/chinas-central-bank-buys-gold-15th-consecutive-month-2026-02-07/).

"This group has significantly grown and now includes leading states in Eurasia, Africa, the Middle East, and Latin America...The BRICS countries account for not only a third of the Earth's landmass and almost half the planet's population, but also for 40 percent of the global economy, while their combined GDP at purchasing power parity stands at $77 trillion. This is the 2025 data according to the IMF. By the way, BRICS is substantially ahead of other groups in this parameter, including G7 with $57 trillion...

Year after year, our group's global authority and influence continue growing. BRICS has rightfully established itself as one of the key centres of global governance, with our collective voice in support of the global majority's vital interests resonating ever more powerfully across the international stage.

We all see that the world is experiencing tectonic shifts. The unipolar system of international relations that once served the interests of the so-called golden billion, is losing its relevance, replaced by a more just multi-polar world. Global economic patterns are changing faster. Everything indicates that the liberal globalisation model is becoming obsolete while the centre of business activity is gravitating towards developing markets, launching a powerful growth wave, including in the BRICS countries. To maximise the emerging prospects, it is important to intensify cooperation within the group, primarily in technology, effective resource development, logistics, insurance, trade and finance."

VLADIMIR PUTIN (PRESIDENT OF RUSSIA),
JULY 6TH 2025 AT THE PLENARY SESSION OF THE 17TH
BRICS SUMMIT

CHAPTER 02

O

Owning Gold & Silver Allows You to Have Tangible Assets That Do Not Have Counterparty Risks

When You Buy Silver & Gold, What Should You Do With It?

- When you decide to invest in silver and gold, all you need to do is hold.

- You could spend your day polishing your silver and gold.

- You could put your gold into a pot so that you could have a "pot of gold."

- You could check the price of silver and gold frantically throughout the day.

NOTABLE QUOTABLE

"If you look at it just from a strategic asset-allocation perspective, you would probably have something like 15% of your portfolio in gold, because it is one asset that does very well when the typical parts of the portfolio go down."

RAY DALIO

(Raymond Thomas Dalio (born August 8, 1949) is an American billionaire and hedge fund manager, who has been co-chief investment officer of Bridgewater Associates since 1985. As of December 2024, Dalio ranks #124 on Forbes' Richest People in the World with a net worth of $15.4 billion. He founded Bridgewater in 1975 in his New York City two-bedroom apartment. Dalio was born in New York City and attended C.W. Post College of Long Island University before receiving an MBA from Harvard Business School in 1973. In 2013, Bridgewater was listed as the largest hedge fund in the world. Dalio is the author of the 2017 book, Principles: Life & Work, about corporate management and investment philosophy and The Changing World Order on why Nations succeed and fail.)

If Buying Silver & Gold Is Such a Consistent Investment Why Don't More People Buy Gold and Silver?

Most people (the majority) are wrong about most things most of the time. Take a moment to consider the following FUN FACTS as proof.

- Most people are wrong about business - "96% of businesses fail." - https://www.inc.com/bill-carmody/why-96-of-businesses-fail-within-10-years.html

- Most people are wrong about theft - "75% of employees have stolen from their employer at least once, according to the U.S. Chamber of Commerce." - https://www.forbes.com/sites/ivywalker/2018/12/28/your-employees-are-probably-stealing-from-you-here-are-five-ways-to-put-an-end-to-it/

- Most people are wrong about honesty - "85% of job applicants lie on resumes." - https://www.inc.com/jt-odonnell/staggering-85-of-job-applicants-lying-on-resumes-.html

Is Buying Silver & Gold a Safe Haven?

Gold and silver are considered to be a "safe haven" by most financial experts.

What Is a "Safe Haven" Asset?

- A "Safe Haven" asset is an asset that in times of economic turmoil, decline, and uncertainty, historically maintains its value.

- Shockingly, a "Shake Weight" is not deemed to be a "Safe Haven" asset.

How Much Cash Should You Keep On Hand During Times of Economic Gloom or Boom?

Although cash will lose value through inflation, it can be difficult to buy a new computer from Best Buy using silver coins and to buy burritos from Chipotle using gold coins. Thus, we believe everyone should have some cash on hand to weather the daily transactions and storms that life throws at you. Many experts recommend having three to six months' worth of cash on hand at all times.

FUN FACT:

When the Mexican businessman Zhenli Ye Gon was arrested with $207 million in both cash and pesos on hand, he claimed that it was being used for a political campaign. However, the cash turned out to be related to drug trafficking.

How Safe Is Gold And Silver?

- Gold and silver are one of the only assets in the world that do not have a counterparty risk.

- Gold and silver have had monetary and industrial use and value since the beginning of recorded history.

What Is Counterparty Risk?

- Counterparty risk (or counterparty credit risk) is the statistical probability that one party in a financial transaction will default on the agreement and their contractual obligations. (The business fails, the sales slow down, the economy falls apart, the brother-in-law impregnates an employee and then attempts to start a business to compete with you, your partner embezzles cash, the market changes, etc.) Counterparty risk involves the reality of experiencing a potential loss due to non-payment, failure to honor an agreement, or failure to deliver assets.

- Lending money to a brother-in-law who has a history of financial "jackassery" would be an example of an investment with massive amounts of counterparty risk.

- Lending money to a man who watches Andrew Tate videos as a source of wisdom and life advice would be an example of an investment with massive amounts of counterparty risk.

- Investing in a gold mine located in communist China (who has the habit of seizing assets) would be an example of an investment with massive amounts of counterparty risk.

- Gold and silver are the only major assets in the world without counterparty risk. Gold and silver are assets that humanity has used for thousands of years and they provide investors unique dual qualities of being both a solid investment (that is actually viewed internationally as a form of currency) to protect your wealth against inflation and being increasingly used within industry.

NOTABLE QUOTABLE

"It may be too late to save the dollar, but it is not too late to preserve wealth. We live in an ersatz monetary system that has reached its end stage."

JAMES G. RICKARDS,
THE DEATH OF MONEY: THE COMING COLLAPSE OF THE INTERNATIONAL MONETARY SYSTEM.

(James G. Rickards is an American lawyer, economist, investment banker, speaker, media commentator, and author on matters of finance and precious metals. He graduated from Johns Hopkins University in 1973 with a Bachelor of Arts degree with honors, and in 1974, from the Paul H. Nitze School of Advanced International Studies in Washington, D.C., with an M.A. in international economics. He received his Juris Doctor from the University of Pennsylvania Law School and a Master of Laws in taxation from New York University School of Law. He has held senior positions at Citibank, Long-Term Capital Management, and Caxton Associates. Rickards worked on Wall Street for 35 years.)

What Are the Risks of Investing In Stocks?

Whenever you decide to invest in buying stock, you are literally buying (or investing in) the success or failure of a business. As a business owner myself, I have never felt comfortable investing in another business that I have no control over, when I could either invest in my own business (which I have control over), or in gold and silver which have virtually no counterparty risk.

When you invest in a stock, if the business performs poorly, then the stock you invested in will not succeed. As a general rule, a successful company is profitable. Profits are what keeps a company going and growing. If a company does not make a profit they will fail. If the business you invested in loses money quarter after quarter, it will ultimately go into bankruptcy and the stock you invested in will be worth zero. Regardless of how bad the economy is, it is very difficult, if not impossible, for gold and silver to become worth zero.

What Are the Risks of Investing In Bonds?

When the stock market is experiencing extreme volatility, investors often want to dive into bonds. Whether it be major corporate banks, municipal bonds, or (what many consider to be the safest bonds) U.S. Treasury bonds are generally considered by most investors to be a safe investment and a safer investment than stocks during times of economic chaos and recession.

However, since the COVID related lockdowns, quarantines, curfews and mandates, I believe we are living in ULTRA PREMIUM EXTREME TIMES OF FINANCIAL CHAOS. Thus, when I think about bonds, I think about their counterparty risk. I think about what could happen that could make the bonds worth less or worthless. Remember, a bond is an asset for you if you are a bond buyer and are basically a creditor to the organizations that now owe money to you. However, what if the organization or government that owes you money collapses? Think about this for a second. Our government is printing a trillion dollars of new debt every three months. We live in times of unsustainable-mind-blowing-compounding government debt and the self-proclaimed "King of Debt" (President Donald J. Trump) is our president. Thus, I prefer to buy silver and gold and hold.

NOTABLE QUOTABLE

"Compound interest is the eighth wonder of the world. He who understands it, earns it... he who doesn't, pays it."

ALBERT EINSTEIN

(Albert Einstein (14 March 1879 – 18 April 1955) was a German-born theoretical physicist best known for developing the theory of relativity. Einstein also made important contributions to quantum theory. His mass–energy equivalence formula $E = mc2$, which arises from special relativity, has been called "the world's most famous equation". He received the 1921 Nobel Prize in Physics for "his services to theoretical physics, and especially for his discovery of the law of the photoelectric effect".)

NOTABLE QUOTABLE

"I'm the king of debt. I'm great with debt. Nobody knows debt better than me...I've made a fortune by using debt, and if things don't work out I renegotiate the debt. I mean, that's a smart thing, not a stupid thing."

PRESIDENT DONALD J. TRUMP

https://www.politico.com/story/2016/06/trump-king-of-debt-224642

NOTABLE QUOTABLE

"The rich ruleth over the poor, and the borrower is servant to the lender."

PROVERBS 22:7

(Proverbs was written by King Solomon. King Solomon prayed relentlessly that God would give him wisdom. Under King Solomon's leadership, Israel reached the peak of its wealth. However, King Solomon also did not listen to everything God told him because he went on to have 700 wives and 300 concubines. If you are reading this, I would encourage you to not have 700 wives and 300 concubines.)

What Are the Risks of Investing In ETFS (Exchange-Traded Funds) and Mutual Funds?

First off, what is an ETF? An ETF is an exchange-traded fund. This fund is an investment fund that will hold a variety of assets, like stock and bonds on the stock exchange just like common stock. ETFs are sold as a way to offer diversification by putting together many investments into a single fund that can be bought and sold through a typical day.

What Are Mutual Funds?

Mutual funds are a financial vehicle which allows many investors to pool their money together into a diversified portfolio of stocks, bonds, and other securities. These funds are allegedly managed by professionals who are focused on helping the fund to achieve their financial goals. Investors into these funds buy shares of the investment fund, which then represent having a part ownership of the entire portfolio and the overall wins and losses that this fund experiences. I personally would never want to pool my money with my neighbors, my friends, or any group of people to share in our combined wins and losses.

The ETFs and mutual funds that people invest in are ultimately only as good as the specific assets which they own. Thus, if the ETF does not own successful investments, the fund will not do well. If you own a mutual fund, which owns stocks and bonds that are performing well then your ETF will do well. I personally do not like ETFs and mutual funds because they involve counterparty risk. And at the risk of not being redundant enough...as a business owner myself, I have NEVER felt comfortable investing in another business that I have no control over when I could either invest in my own business (which I have control over), or in gold and silver which have virtually no counterparty risk. Do ETFs and mutual funds involve counterparty risk? Yes! Thus, I buy silver and gold and hold.

What Are the Risks of Investing In Cash and Bank Investments?

Although many people may not agree with me, I know that inflation is a very real form of counterparty risk. Inflation simply means that more and more money is being printed by the United States government to buy things that they cannot afford. Every time more and more water (money) is poured into our orange juice (currency), the orange juice begins to taste more and more watered down (our money is worth less) as it becomes more and more diluted and watered down because it is more and more diluted and watered down.

When governments print more and more money, this causes the price of everything to increase. Inflation is terrible and very real. So what is the counterparty risk involved in currency? We now live in a time where our government on both sides of the political aisle (Democrats and Republicans) demonstrate on a daily basis that they have no problem with spending more money than we have while causing epic amounts of inflation.

NOTABLE QUOTABLE

"Inflation is taxation without legislation."

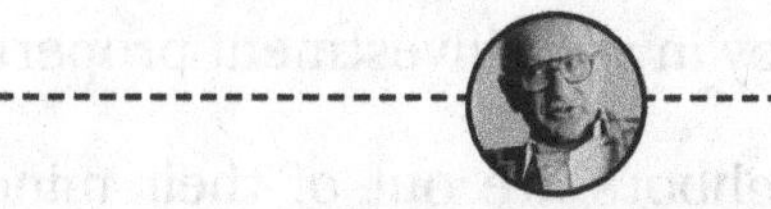

MILTON FRIEDMAN

(Milton Friedman (July 31, 1912 – November 16, 2006) was a legendary American economist and statistician who received the 1976 Nobel Memorial Prize in Economic Sciences for his research on consumption analysis, monetary history and theory and the complexity of stabilization policy.)

What Are the Risks of Investing In Real Estate?

As a business owner, I personally choose to invest in the following two ways only.

1. I buy undervalued real estate and I wait.

2. I buy silver and gold and I hold.

However, I want everyone reading this to understand that when you invest in real estate there are MASSIVE AMOUNTS OF COUNTERPARTY RISKS INVOLVED INCLUDING:

1. What if your renter chooses not to pay?

2. What if you have a leaking shower in your property that needs to be fixed?

3. What if you have an appliance that needs to be replaced?

4. What if your ice maker leaks and floods the house?

5. What if your investment property gets vandalized?

6. What if an ambitious homeless community decides to take up residency in your investment property?

7. What if your neighbors are out of their minds (perhaps your neighbors have multiple minds) and they make your property unusable for your real estate's intended use?

8. What if you deal with nefarious contractors that take advantage of you, overcharge you, and fail to deliver the result you paid them to achieve?

9. What if the man building your investment property dies on a motorcycle?

10. What if geopolitical issues that are out of your control make your investment property undesirable?

11. What if you cannot find a good property management service?

12. What if you cannot find a cleaning service that you can trust?

13. What if your neighbor makes your property unattractive because they are turning their property into a reenactment of the "Burning Man" festival filled with sex, drugs, and loud music?

14. What if crime becomes prevalent in the area surrounding your property?

15. What if the communists parachute in from the sky to take over our country, like in Red Dawn starring Patrick Swayze?

16. What if our country experiences civil unrest or war?

17. What if your community gets bombed?

18. I don't have any hard data on it, but I bet the value of real estate went down in the communities being bombed by the Germans during World War II.

19. What happens if mass illegal immigration happens near your home? I don't have the hard facts in front of me, but I am pretty sure that the value of the homes located along the United States and Mexico border have been impacted by the very active and consistent flow of illegal immigration and the crime and drug culture that comes with it.

What Are the Risks of Investing In Cryptocurrency?

I believe you should read this patent in its entirety before making your decision as to whether you should invest in cryptocurrency or not.

PATENT: WO-2020-060606-A1 - Cryptocurrency system using body activity data - READ - https://patents.google.com/patent/WO2020060606A1/en

NOTABLE QUOTABLE

"It's important not to think about Bitcoin as a replacement for cash or gold or something that works alongside that; it's to think of it as programmable money. And we just cannot even imagine what that will be used for."

NAVAL RAVIKANT

(Naval Ravikant (born November 5, 1974) is an Indian-born American entrepreneur and investor. He is the co-founder and chairman of AngelList, a platform for startups, investors, and job seekers. He is an angel investor who has made early-stage investments in companies including Uber, Twitter, Postmates, and Yammer. Ravikant is a recipient of the Edmund Hillary Fellowship. He also co-hosts a podcast with Brett Hall.)

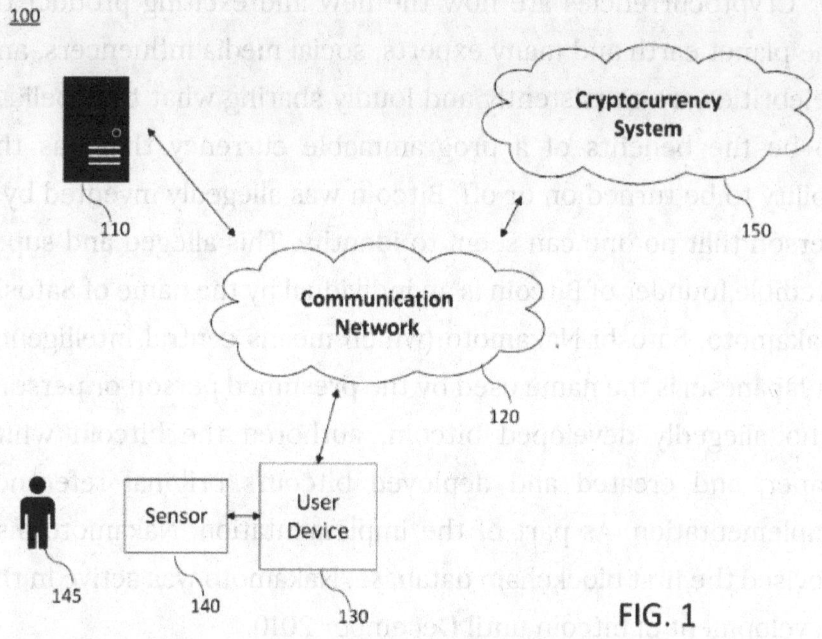

Abstract for Patent WO/2020/060606

Human body activity associated with a task provided to a user may be used in a mining process of a cryptocurrency system. A server may provide a task to a device of a user which is communicatively coupled to the server. A sensor communicatively coupled to or comprised in the device of the user may sense body activity of the user. Body activity data may be generated based on the sensed body activity of the user. The cryptocurrency system communicatively coupled to the device of the user may verify if the body activity data satisfies one or more conditions set by the cryptocurrency system, and award cryptocurrency to the user whose body activity data is verified.

Cryptocurrencies are now the new and exciting product on the planet earth and many experts, social media influencers, and celebrities are consistently and loudly sharing what they believe to be the benefits of a programmable currency that has the ability to be turned on or off. Bitcoin was allegedly invented by a person that no one can seem to identify. This alleged and super credible founder of Bitcoin is an individual by the name of Satoshi Nakamoto. Satoshi Nakamoto (which means central intelligence in Japanese) is the name used by the presumed person or persons who allegedly developed bitcoin, authored the bitcoin white paper, and created and deployed bitcoin's original reference implementation. As part of the implementation, Nakamoto also devised the first blockchain database. Nakamoto was active in the development of bitcoin until December 2010.

FUN FACT:

In case you missed it! BREAKING NEWS!!! In Japanese, "Satoshi" (聡) often means "wise," "intelligent," or "clear," while "Nakamoto" (中本) translates to "middle" or "central origin" (Naka = middle, Moto = origin/base).

From my perspective the PATENT: W0-2020-060606-A1 for a Cryptocurrency system using body activity data sounds very much like Revelation chapter 13 verse 16 through 18.

NOTABLE QUOTABLE

"16 And he causeth all, both small and great, rich and poor, free and bond, to receive a mark in their right hand, or in their foreheads: 17 And that no man might buy or sell, save he that had the mark, or the name of the beast, or the number of his name. 18 Here is wisdom. Let him that hath understanding count the number of the beast: for it is the number of a man; and his number is Six hundred threescore and six."

REVELATION 13:16-18

(The Book of Revelation was written by a man named John, who was one of the twelve Apostles of Jesus Christ. John the Apostle wrote the Book of Revelation while exiled on the island of Patmos around 95–96 (AD – After the Death, Resurrection and Ascension of our Lord and Savior Jesus Christ).)

However, the counterparty risks that I see with cryptocurrency are:

- Electronic Hacking from someone or some nation with the technical skills needed to get into digital assets and steal it.

- Electricity (And Or a Lack There Of) is essential for cryptocurrency to work. If electricity is not available, then your cryptocurrency is not available.

Over the years, there have been many, many examples and cases of good people who had their cryptocurrency accounts go all the way to zero because of fraud and various other issues that my mind cannot comprehend.

Remember, cryptocurrencies are entirely dependent on the assumption that we shall always have an ABUNDANCE OF ELECTRICITY, which in turn means that all cryptocurrency is worth zero during the times of a blackout. As an added bonus thought: Who was the Bitcoin founder, Satoshi Nakamoto? Was Satoshi Nakamoto a real human? Was Satoshi Nakamoto a good guy? Gold was allegedly founded by God. Who is God?

"Nobody can explain to me who Satoshi Nakamoto
was? The creator of Bitcoin? This mysterious
guy? Who apparently died but nobody knew who
he was?...CIA? That's my guess. I can't prove it.
You are telling me to invest in something whose
founder is mysterious and has billions of dollars
of unused Bitcoin? Like what is that? And no one
can answer that question including some of the
biggest holders of Bitcoin in the world who I know
personally. And they are like oh it doesn't matter.
Well it matters to me."

TUCKER CARLSON

(Speaking at Turning Point - October 21st 2025)

DID YOU KNOW THAT SATOSHI NAKAMOTO MEANS "CENTRAL INTELLIGENCE" IN JAPANESE?

» "Satoshi Nakamoto" (中本哲史) is a common Japanese name that, when broken down means:
  ◦ Satoshi = Intelligence
  ◦ Nakamoto = Central

Although everybody on the planet would like to become wealthy quickly and to "get rich quick" that is not the primary reason that anyone should be investing in the buying of gold and silver. People that typically stretch out and reach for BIG FAST GAINS typically end up experiencing PAINFUL FAST LOSSES. The purpose of buying gold is to protect your wealth. Buying gold is like buying an insurance policy to protect your wealth against inflation caused by a government obsessed with spending money that it does not have on things that it cannot afford. If you choose to invest in buying gold and silver you need to be disciplined. You cannot let your emotions overrule your long-term plan of buying gold and silver to protect your wealth. If the day-to-day price of gold and silver goes up or down today this should not impact your decision to invest in or not invest in the buying of gold and silver.

"In the absence of the gold standard, there is no way to protect savings from confiscation through inflation. There is no safe store of value."

ALAN GREENSPAN

(Is an American economist who served as the 13th chairman of the Federal Reserve from 1987 to 2006. He worked as a private adviser and provided consulting for firms through his company, Greenspan Associates LLC. First nominated to the Federal Reserve by President Ronald Reagan in August 1987, Greenspan was reappointed at successive four-year intervals until retiring on January 31, 2006, after the second-longest tenure in the position, behind only William McChesney Martin.)

NOTABLE QUOTABLE

"Cryptocurrency equals control. Gold equals security. Gold equals financial security. People are very private about gold investing. But, you don't want to tell people exactly what you are doing."

GENERAL FLYNN

CHAPTER 03

L

Liquid Assets Such As Gold Allow You To Be Financially Malleable

What Are the Risks of Owning Silver and Gold?

When you invest in silver and gold, you shall experience the following risks and more:

- **Theft:** When you own physical silver and gold, you could have it stolen.

- **Government Seizure:** Many people forget, but during the Great Depression, gold ownership by private citizens was banned by our socialist President Franklin D. Roosevelt's administration (and his allegedly lesbian wife), who actually implemented gold confiscation as his official policy.

Communist governments and socialist governments have a long history of seizing private property by simply declaring that they are going to be "nationalizing" or "socializing" a specific asset.

- **Your Brother-In-Law:** You may have a nefarious brother-in-law that you don't trust because they are not trustworthy. When your investment strategy involves: Buy silver and gold then hold; this kind of strategy may become tempting to the criminal mind of your extended family.

- If you aren't paying attention, you could get hit by a train. In 2024: 954 total deaths happened as a result of railroad-related accidents.

- If you aren't watching yourself and looking out for danger at all times, you could get struck by lightning. From 2006 through 2021, there were 444 lighting strike deaths in the United States. - READ - https://www.cdc.gov/lightning/data-research/index.html#:~:text=From%202006%20through%202021%2C%20there,to%20be%20struck%20by%20lightning.

- Unless you wear a helmet to bed every night, you could fall right out of bed and die. Estimated Annual Deaths: Around 450 people die from falling out of bed each year in the US, according to multiple sources.

- Unless you wisely choose to live in a below ground bunker at all times, you could get violently sucked up in an Oklahoma tornado. In fact, in 2015 a mind-blowing 2 people died as a result of tornados in Oklahoma. In fact in 2011, a SHOCKING total of 14 people died as a result of being sucked up by an Oklahoma tornado! - READ - https://en.wikipedia.org/wiki/Tornadoes_in_ Oklahoma

NOTABLE QUOTABLE

"Gold serves a purpose. It is first of all, a diversifier against other assets... it's a diversifying asset that is sensible, and that's the main reason to have gold in the portfolio, five to 10%."

RAY DALIO

(Raymond Thomas Dalio (born August 8, 1949) is an American billionaire and hedge fund manager, who has been co-chief investment officer of Bridgewater Associates since 1985. As of December 2024, Dalio ranks #124 on Forbes' Richest People in the World with a net worth of $15.4 billion. He founded Bridgewater in 1975 in his New York City two-bedroom apartment. Dalio was born in New York City and attended C.W. Post College of Long Island University before receiving an MBA from Harvard Business School in 1973. In 2013, Bridgewater was listed as the largest hedge fund in the world. Dalio is the author of the 2017 book, Principles: Life & Work, about corporate management and investment philosophy and The Changing World Order on why Nations succeed and fail.)

NOTABLE QUOTABLE

"Deficit spending is simply a scheme for the
'hidden' confiscation of wealth. Gold stands in
the way of this insidious process. It stands as a
protector of property rights."

ALAN GREENSPAN

*(Alan Greenspan is an American economist who served as the 13th
chairman of the Federal Reserve from 1987 to 2006. He worked as a
private adviser and provided consulting for firms through his company,
Greenspan Associates LLC. First nominated to the Federal Reserve by
President Ronald Reagan in August 1987, Greenspan was reappointed
at successive four-year intervals until retiring on January 31, 2006,
after the second-longest tenure in the position, behind only William
McChesney Martin.)*

Much like silver, gold has monetary value as a medium of
exchange, and has an industrial value because gold is being
increasingly used within the industry.

Gold has incredible industrial uses that leverage gold's mind-
blowing conductivity, resistance to corrosion, and reflectivity,
primarily in electronics (connectors, circuits in phones,
computers, cars), and aerospace (satellite coatings, astronaut
helmets), medicine (dentistry, drug delivery). Gold is used as a
catalyst in chemical manufacturing, and it is commonly used in
jewelry and finance.

NOTABLE QUOTABLE

"Gold is money. Everything else is credit."

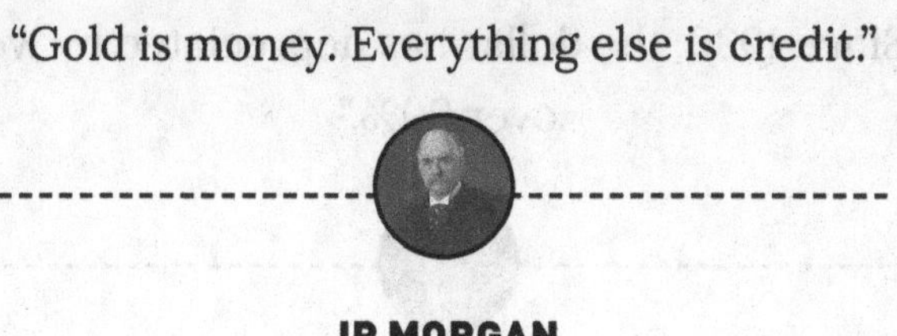

JP MORGAN

(John Pierpont Morgan Sr. (April 17, 1837 – March 31, 1913) was an American financier and investment banker who dominated corporate finance on Wall Street throughout the Gilded Age and Progressive Era. As the head of the banking firm that ultimately became known as JPMorgan Chase & Co., he was a driving force behind the wave of industrial consolidations in the United States at the turn of the twentieth century. Over the course of his career on Wall Street, Morgan spearheaded the formation of several prominent multinational corporations including U.S. Steel, International Harvester, and General Electric. He and his partners also held controlling interests in numerous other American businesses including Aetna, Western Union, the Pullman Car Company, and 21 railroads. His grandfather Joseph Morgan was one of the co-founders of Aetna. Through his holdings, Morgan exercised enormous influence over capital markets in the United States. During the Panic of 1907, he organized a coalition of financiers that saved the American monetary system from collapse.)

What Are the Risks of Saving Money In a Bank?

When you deposit your money into a bank, your money is losing value every day if the interest the bank pays you for investing your money into the bank is not greater than the rate of inflation.

Let me repeat. When you deposit your money into a bank, your money is losing value every day if the interest the bank pays you for investing your money into the bank is not greater than the rate of inflation.

NOTABLE QUOTABLE

"Since 1930, the dollar has depreciated by well
over 90%."

WARREN BUFFETT

*(Warren Edward Buffett is an American investor and philanthropist
who is the chairman and former CEO of the conglomerate Berkshire
Hathaway. As a result of his success, Buffett is one of the best-known
investors in America. According to Forbes, as of January 2026, Buffett's
estimated net worth stood at US$148.9 billion, making him the ninth-
richest individual in the world.)*

When you decide to put your money into an FDIC-insured bank, you and I have the belief that the FDIC will insure your deposits up to $250,000. However, what is the FDIC? FDIC stands for the Federal Deposit Insurance Corporation. This Federal Deposit Insurance Corporation is an independent U.S. government agency that was created in 1933 to help maintain the stability and overall confidence of the public in America's financial system. However, the Federal Reserve is not federal, and there is no reserve.

NOTABLE QUOTABLE

"The accepted version of history is that the Federal
Reserve was created to stabilize our economy. One
of the most widely-used textbooks on this subject
says: "It sprang from the panic of 1907, with its
alarming epidemic of bank failures: the country
was fed up once and for all with the anarchy of
unstable private banking." 23 Even the most naive
student must sense a grave contradiction between
this cherished view and the System's actual
performance. Since its inception, it has presided
over the crashes of 1921 and 1929; the Great
Depression of '29 to '39; recessions in '53, '57, '69,
'75, and '81; a stock market "Black Monday" in '87;
and a 1000% inflation which has destroyed 90% of
the dollar's purchasing power.24"

G. EDWARD GRIFFIN

*(G. Edward Griffin is the best-selling author of The Creature from Jekyll
Island: A Second Look at the Federal Reserve.)*

Today, if your local bank were to fail they actually have the authority to take your money to cover the bank's liabilities via a concept known as bail-ins. The Great Recession experience that all Americans lived through ushered in a new concept known as "too big to fail." The belief of "too big to fail" was that the United States government had an obligation to rescue some of the largest financial institutions through taxpayer-funded bailouts. Then in 2010, the United States Congress passed what is known as the Dodd-Frank Wall Street Reform and Consumer Act, which eliminated the option of providing bank bailouts in the future while opening the door for a new concept known as "bail-ins."

NOTABLE QUOTABLE

"The market needs to set prices, including interest
rates and allocate resources. If it were up to
me, we would abolish the Fed and return to the
gold standard. Absent that, the Fed should be
completely removed from the political sphere,
its dual mandate replaced by a single mission to
provide the nation with sound money."

PETER SCHIFF

*(Peter David Schiff is an American stockbroker, financial commentator,
and radio personality. He co-founded Echelon Wealth Partners in
Canada (formerly Euro Pacific Canada). He is involved in other
financial services companies including Euro Pacific Asset Management,
as an independent investment advisor, and Schiff Gold (formerly
Euro Pacific Precious Metals). He has criticized US banking and credit
practices.)*

What Are Bail-Ins?

Bail-ins are allegedly designed to help prevent the complete and total collapse of a bank that is failing due to what I call "financial jackassery." Bail-ins create a scenario where the person who deposits their money at the bank now bails the burden for rescuing their bank if their bank is failing. Think about it! If your bank begins to fail, you could become the hero that successfully uses all of your money to save your bank with your bail-in!

During a bailout, the government injects money and capital into a struggling bank, which allows the struggling bank to continue operating. During the great financial crisis of 2007-2008, the United States government used your tax payer dollars to inject $700 billion into massive companies like Bank of America (BAC), Citigroup (C), and American International Group (AIG)!

However, now that bail-ins are legal, your deposited money can be used to provide immediate relief to a struggling bank. Thus, banks can now use money from their unsecured creditors (you), including depositors (you) and bondholders (potentially you), to restructure their capital. Banks can convert their debt into equity to increase their capital requirements. Does this make sense? Does this make you nauseous? Does this make you cautious? Does this make you want to buy silver and gold and just put it in your closet?

Although I believe that buying silver and gold is a great venue for me to invest, I do know that it will be very difficult for you to buy your groceries from Whole Foods this week with your silver coins, and the knowledge that I am providing within the beautiful pages of this beautiful book. Thus, you need to have some cash savings available in addition to whatever silver and gold investments you decide to make.

NOTABLE QUOTABLE

"If you owe the bank $100, that's your problem. If
you owe the bank $100 million, that's the bank's
problem."

J. PAUL GETTY

*(Jean Paul Getty Sr. (December 15, 1892 – June 6, 1976) was an American
petroleum industrialist who founded the Getty Oil Company in 1942
and was the patriarch of the Getty family. A native of Minneapolis,
Minnesota, he was the son of pioneer oilman George Getty. In
1957, Fortune magazine named J. Paul Getty the wealthiest living
American. The 1966 Guinness Book of Records declared him to be the
world's wealthiest private citizen, worth an estimated $1.2 billion
(approximately $8.8 billion in 2024). At the time of his death, he was
worth more than $6 billion (approximately $26 billion in 2024). A book
published in 1996 ranked him as the 67th wealthiest American who
ever lived (based on his wealth as a percentage of the concurrent gross
national product.)*

What Are the Physical Risks With Investing In Silver & Gold Ownership?

If somebody gets mad at you and they know the location
of where you keep your precious metals, they could pick up a
silver coin, a silver ingot, or a gold bar, and throw it at you! If
you own enough silver and gold, you could injure your back while
attempting to pick up your pallets of them.

Also, when you own gold and silver, you must come to grips
with the idea that you now own valuable property that people
without integrity would like to steal, to take, and to make their
own. Thus, you want to make sure that you find a secure location

for your precious metals. You can decide whether you want to store your precious metals somewhere buried in your lawn, in a safety deposit box at the local bank, in a third-party vault, in your attic, in a safe, or somewhere else altogether. Who knows... maybe buying gold and silver will inspire you to build a do-it-yourself underground bunker to safely store your silver and gold. My friend, there are many reputable vendors out there that specialize in safely storing silver and gold investments. But you have to make a decision about where you are going to safely store your precious metals. I would highly recommend not shouting about how much gold and silver you own at your local restaurant or sharing how much gold and silver you own during a moment of irrational emotionally-inspired candor while hanging out with a bunch of people you just met during a campfire soul-cleansing conversation at ministry camp.

What Are the Risks of Investing In Anything Ever?

The concept of investing relates to you buying an asset that you believe will increase in value over time. To help clear up any confusion here, I have provided the following examples:

- Investing your money into a fast-growing tech stock that came out of nowhere and is "headed to the moon" is a very risky investment.

- Investing your money in the stocks of "can't miss" gold and silver mining companies that you know very little about is a very risky investment.

- Investing your money into lending your family and friends any amount of money ever is a very risky investment.

- Investing your money into silver and gold certificates as opposed to investing in the ownership and possession of actual physical silver and gold is a very risky investment.

- Investing your money into paying a person (with a history of being flaky and watching Andrew Tate videos) to learn how to train dogs at a high-level so that you can continue to make a percentage of their gross earnings until they pay you back is a very risky investment.

- Investing your money into any business that your multiple-times divorced and perpetually broken brother-in-law wants to start is a very risky investment.

- Investing your money into the concept of flipping houses with a college student and a contractor you just met is a very risky investment.

- Investing your money into the concept of allowing a man in his late 40s to move into your office without paying rent so that he can pay you a percentage of his future earnings that you will teach him how to produce is a very risky investment.

NOTABLE QUOTABLE

"[19]Lay not up for yourselves treasures upon earth, where moth and rust doth corrupt, and where thieves break through and steal: [20]But lay up for yourselves treasures in heaven, where neither moth nor rust doth corrupt, and where thieves do not break through nor steal."

MATTHEW 6:19-20

(Matthew was a book written by one of Jesus' twelve Apostles. Most scholars believe that Matthew was martyred (murdered and killed) with a sword because he would not renounce his faith.)

FUN FACTS:

» Approximately 100% of people born on Earth will die. Thus, I wouldn't spend too much time thinking about how to store my riches while living on the planet Earth. However, the Bible does discuss the concept of being raptured and a few people that were raptured throughout history:

» Genesis Chapter 5:24 states that Enoch was raptured.

» The Bible does state in 2 Kings 2:11 and Hebrews 11:7 that Elijah was raptured.

» In the New Testament, the Bible does state that The Spirit of the Lord "caught away" Philip to another location after he baptized the Ethiopian eunuch, as seen in Acts 8:39.

» Jesus was raptured in Luke 24 and Acts 1.

» In the New Testament, the Bible also discusses Paul being "caught up" to the third heaven in 2 Corinthians 12:2-4.

» The Bible also discusses the future prophetic rapture of the church in 1 Thessalonians 4:16-17.

» In Revelation Chapter 11, the Bible also describes the future ascension of "The Two Witnesses" during the tribulation.

What Does the Word Rapture Mean?

The Rapture is a belief held amongst Bible-reading Christians that believers (both living and dead) will be suddenly "caught up" or "snatched away" from Earth to meet Jesus Christ in the air at the time of His second coming. The concept of "The Rapture" is described in 1 Thessalonians 4:16-17 and 1 Corinthians 15:50-54. Although the word "rapture" itself is not found in the Bible, the concept comes from the Latin word meaning "to snatch away."

Do Banks Actually Keep Your Deposits On Hand?

Our American banking system is based on fractionalized banking. Fractionalized banking is a concept that the average American does not understand. In fact, most Americans would find the concept of fractionalized banking IMPOSSIBLE TO BELIEVE. Think about fractionalized banking like this: If a depositor (customer) at the bank deposits one thousand dollars into the bank using our current fractionalized banking system, how much money can the bank lend out to others?

Most people would believe that the bank is only available to lend out some amount less than the one thousand dollars that was deposited, right? However, the way fractionalized banking works, the bank can now lend out an additional $8,000 or $9,000 to someone other than the customer who deposited $1,000. Banks literally have the power to lend out money that they do not have. Banks are literally able to lend out multiples of the money that has been invested into the bank. Using the fractionalized "magic money" banking system, banks are now able to lend out many times more money than they ever had on hand to begin with as a result of deposits. Does this make sense? Well it doesn't. In the fractionalized banking system, if the bank has one dollar deposited, it can lend out nine dollars. This, my friend, is how the fractionalized banking system works!

The average American has no idea how our fractionalized banking system works, and the average American leader has no idea how the fractionalized "magic money" banking system works. If the average person ever understood the concept that banks could lend out more money than they ever had in the form of deposits their brains might figuratively explode. There would also be a run on the banks as depositors would rush to their local bank to attempt to get their actual money out of the bank that is in the business of lending money it does not have.

NOTABLE QUOTABLE

"I want to just obey the Constitution.The
Constitution says only gold and silver can be legal
tender."

RON PAUL

*(Ronald Ernest Paul (born August 20, 1935) is an American author,
activist, medical doctor, and former politician who served as the U.S.
representative for Texas's 22nd congressional district from 1976 to 1977,
and again from 1979 to 1985, as well as for Texas's 14th congressional
district from 1997 to 2013. On three occasions, he sought the presidency
of the United States, first as the Libertarian Party nominee in 1988, and
then as a candidate for the Republican Party in 2008 and 2012.)*

What Are the Risks of Trading?

Trading is the most common way and the short-term for those
that choose to invest in stocks throughout the day based upon
their knowledge of specific stocks and their current price relative
to their actual value. If you choose to become a day trader, you
must have incredibly calm nerves and the mental ability to pull the
trigger quickly when a great detail becomes available. Personally, I
believe that becoming a bomb defuser and an explosive ordnance
disposal specialist for the Iranian government seems less risky
than becoming a day trader. If you do decide to become a trader,
you need to look at the money you are choosing to invest as risk
capital and not money that you need for emergencies, for daily
life, for paying your rent, for retiring, and for feeding yourself.

FUN FACT:

"Gold is a 'noble' metal, meaning it doesn't rust, tarnish, corrode, or lose its shine when exposed to air. It also resists reacting with acids, which is why ancient gold artifacts still gleam today. And while gold can be melted, reshaped, or alloyed, the gold atoms themselves aren't destroyed—that would require a nuclear reaction. In short, all the gold ever mined still exists in some form." - https://www.pbs.org/wgbh/masterpiece/specialfeatures/8-fascinating-facts-about-real-gold-that-will-surprise-you/

What is the Risk of Investing 10% of Your Wealth Into the Purchasing of Precious Metals?

Here is a deep thought...If you invest 10% of your investment portfolio into the purchasing of silver and gold you could lose 10% of your investment portfolio.

> "I would say gold is the safest money in this kind of an environment…gold is still the safest…it doesn't change by the day."

RAY DALIO

(Ray Dalio speaking at the February 9th 2026 World Governments Summit: Decisions That Shape Future Governments - Plenary Session. Raymond Thomas Dalio (born August 8, 1949) is an American billionaire and hedge fund manager, who has been co-chief investment officer of Bridgewater Associates since 1985. As of December 2024, Dalio ranks #124 on Forbes' Richest People in the World with a net worth of $15.4 billion. He founded Bridgewater in 1975 in his New York City two-bedroom apartment.) Dalio was born in New York City and attended C.W. Post College of Long Island University before receiving an MBA from Harvard Business School in 1973.)

WATCH - https://www.youtube.com/watch?v=EKpxEQRe_Zc

NOTABLE QUOTABLE

"I think people make the mistake of thinking, 'Is it going to go up or down, and should I buy it?...I think if people were to make — those who are running policies and so on — were to say, they would say gold is the safest money in this kind of environment...Gold is a diversifier. In other words, when the bad times come along, it does uniquely well."

RAY DALIO

(Raymond Thomas Dalio (born August 8, 1949) is an American billionaire and hedge fund manager, who has been co-chief investment officer of Bridgewater Associates since 1985. As of December 2024, Dalio ranks #124 on Forbes' Richest People in the World with a net worth of $15.4 billion. He founded Bridgewater in 1975 in his New York City two-bedroom apartment. Dalio was born in New York City and attended C.W. Post College of Long Island University before receiving an MBA from Harvard Business School in 1973. In 2013, Bridgewater was listed as the largest hedge fund in the world. Dalio is the author of the 2017 book, Principles: Life & Work, about corporate management and investment philosophy and The Changing World Order on why Nations succeed and fail.)

Learn More: https://www.businessinsider.com/ray-dalio-gold-price-crash-safe-haven-investing-advice-2026-2

Back in 2006, a man by the name of Harry Browne died. Who was Harry Browne? Harry Edson Browne (June 17, 1933 – March 1, 2006) was an American writer, libertarian political activist, and investment advisor. He was the Libertarian Party's presidential nominee in the U.S. elections of 1996 and 2000. He authored 12 books that in total have sold more than 2 million copies, including his influential work How I Found Freedom in an Unfree World (1973), which provided a blueprint for achieving individual liberation by rejecting societal constraints and embracing self-reliance. In one of the final books that Harry Browne wrote called Fail-Safe Investing: Lifelong Financial Security In 30 Minutes, he wrote about keeping 25% of your investments in gold. However, you and I are not Harry Browne, and before reading this book you probably didn't know who Harry Browne was.

NOTABLE QUOTABLE

"Don't think about gold as a metal that there
is a speculative mark in it...Think about gold as
a money that central banks treat as a money...
It (gold) is their second (central banks) largest
reserve currency (is gold). It (gold) becomes an
alternative to fiat money."

RAY DALIO

(Raymond Thomas Dalio (born August 8, 1949) is an American billionaire and hedge fund manager, who has been co-chief investment officer of Bridgewater Associates since 1985. As of December 2024, Dalio ranks #124 on Forbes' Richest People in the World with a net worth of $15.4 billion. He founded Bridgewater in 1975 in his New York City two-bedroom apartment. Dalio was born in New York City and attended C.W. Post College of Long Island University before receiving an MBA from Harvard Business School in 1973. In 2013, Bridgewater was listed as the largest hedge fund in the world. Dalio is the author of the 2017 book, Principles: Life & Work, about corporate management and investment philosophy and The Changing World Order on why Nations succeed and fail.)

What is the Risk of Investing In Silver?

Silver has monetary value as a medium of exchange, and it has an industrial value because silver is being increasingly used in the following industries and more:

- Automotive: In engine bearings (plating) and electric vehicle components.

- Batteries: Used as cathode material in rechargeable batteries.

- Biocide: Inhibits bacteria in deodorants, timber preservatives, and hospital surfaces.

- Brazing/Soldering: Creates strong, leak-proof bonds in plumbing, HVAC, and electronics.

- Catalyst: Vital for producing ethylene oxide (plastics, antifreeze) and formaldehyde (resins, adhesives).

- Components: Found in keyboards, speakers, Blu-Ray discs, and 5G network infrastructure.

- Conductivity: Best electrical conductor, used in switches, circuit boards, batteries, and wiring.

- Devices: Applied to catheters, surgical instruments, and implants.

- Electroplating: Used to coat electrical contacts for reliability.

- Nuclear: Used in control rods for nuclear reactors.

- Photography: Historically key for film (silver halides); still used in some X-ray films.

- Solar Panels: Essential in photovoltaic (PV) cells and for reflective coatings.

- Water Purification: Kills bacteria in filters and purification systems.

- Mirrors & Coatings: High reflectivity for specialized mirrors and energy-saving window films.

- Wound Care: Dressings, creams, and coatings prevent infection in burns and chronic wounds.

FUN FACT:

"Most metals are silver or gray, but gold is the only one that's naturally yellow. Copper comes close with a reddish tone and other metals only turn a yellowish color after reacting with air or chemicals. According to the U.S. Geological Survey, pure gold carries a hint of ruby in its glow—a visual uniqueness making it a timeless favorite for currency, jewelry, and art." - https://www.pbs.org/wgbh/masterpiece/specialfeatures/8-fascinating-facts-about-real-gold-that-will-surprise-you/

The fact is that silver's industrial uses are ever-increasing as more and more industries attempt to leverage the conductivity of silver, the antimicrobial properties of silver, and the catalytic abilities of silver electronics. I could write entire books about the EVER-INCREASING uses of silver, but then this book would get too long and my brain might explode! In conclusion, and as I stated above, silver has monetary value as a medium of exchange, and it has an industrial value because silver is being increasingly used in many industries and more: 3D printing, artificial intelligence data centers, automotive, military, solar energy, wart treatment (Yes! Silver is commonly used as an over-the-counter treatment for warts!) water purification, etc.

NOTABLE QUOTABLE

"The Congress should not be creating money out of thin air, which is what Lincoln did when he created greenbacks. But it is a congressional responsibility to maintain gold and silver as a legal tender."

RON PAUL

(Ronald Ernest Paul (born August 20, 1935) is an American author, activist, medical doctor, and former politician who served as the U.S. representative for Texas's 22nd congressional district from 1976 to 1977, and again from 1979 to 1985, as well as for Texas's 14th congressional district from 1997 to 2013. On three occasions, he sought the presidency of the United States, first as the Libertarian Party nominee in 1988, and then as a candidate for the Republican Party in 2008 and 2012.)

What Is the Risk of Investing In Silver Over Gold Or Gold Over Silver?

I do not have an answer for you.

NOTABLE QUOTABLE

"Specie [gold and silver coin] is the most perfect medium because it will preserve its own level; because, having intrinsic and universal value, it can never die in our hands, and it is the surest resource of reliance in time of war."

THOMAS JEFFERSON

(Thomas Jefferson (1743 – July 4th, 1826) was an American Founding Father and the third president of the United States from 1801 to 1809. He was the primary author of the Declaration of Independence. Jefferson was the nation's first U.S. secretary of state under George Washington and then the nation's second vice president under John Adams. Jefferson was a leading proponent of democracy, republicanism, and natural rights, and he produced formative documents and decisions at the state, national, and international levels.)

What is the Risk of Not Investing?

As the United States government continues to print more and more money that it does not have to buy things that it does not need, inflation is only going to increase, and increase exponentially, thus resulting in much higher prices of everything.

As the nations of the world continue to increase the amount of fiat money that they are putting into circulation, the long-term (and maybe near-term) result is going to cause a financial crisis and eventually, will lead to a complete collapse of fiat currencies.

NOTABLE QUOTABLE

"Gold actually has properties – you can use gold for all sorts of things. People value gold for the metal. Nobody values bitcoin for the bitcoin; they value it because they believe that they can exchange it for something else."

PETER SCHIFF

(Peter David Schiff is an American stockbroker, financial commentator, and radio personality. He co-founded Echelon Wealth Partners in Canada (formerly Euro Pacific Canada). He is involved in other financial services companies including Euro Pacific Asset Management, as an independent investment advisor, and Schiff Gold (formerly Euro Pacific Precious Metals). He has criticized US banking and credit practices.)

What Political Risks Relate to Buying Gold & Silver?

Most investors do not think about political risks when investing, however you should. If you ever invest in China, you should know that Communist countries have a habit of seizing assets when they want to, and simply because they can. Most Americans don't know about this or remember this, but in the 1930s right here in these United States of America, our socialist-leaning President Franklin Delano Roosevelt and his wife (who may or may not have been a lesbian) and Congress passed the Gold Reserve Act, which made gold ownership illegal in the United States. Thus, if you bought gold in the years leading up to the Great Depression, you were simply in a bad position. President Roosevelt then issued a presidential order which fixed the price of gold at $35 per ounce. President Roosevelt did not want American citizens to have an alternate form of our currency outside of the United States paper currency, and that is how he got it done. Was it legal? Was it ethical? It didn't and doesn't matter. It happened.

In our world today, this same type of political risk is in the air everywhere. Think about China and Venezuela. These countries routinely "nationalize" properties and take private assets by force, including oil rigs and mining companies. If you owned stock in a mining company that was seized by China or Venezuela, you would have been in a bad spot. As an example, back in the year 2005, the never-corrupt and always kind government of Venezuela mentioned that they were considering seizing the property owned by a Canadian and Toronto-based gold mining company, Crystallex International. As a result, the share price fell by a massive 50% in just one day.

NOTABLE QUOTABLE

"Anything that can go wrong, will go wrong."

EDWARD A. MURPHY JR.

(Murphy's law originated in 1949 at the Edwards Air Force Base during rocket sled tests for human tolerance to G-forces. This concept of Murphy's Law was created by the engineer Edward A. Murphy Jr. after a technician incorrectly installed sensors backward, and was popularized by flight surgeon John Paul Stapp who applied the phrase to the need for rigorous safety planning, turning a complaint into an engineering principle.)

What Is the Risk of Fraud When Investing In Gold And Silver?

When you are investing in gold and silver you want to invest in the purchasing of physical gold and silver. I would highly recommend not investing in gold and silver certificates (which may or may not be real), super-high-markup collector coins, and mining stocks related to companies that you know nothing about.

NOTABLE QUOTABLE

"In the absence of the gold standard, there is no way to protect savings from confiscation through inflation. There is no safe store of value."

ALAN GREENSPAN

(Alan Greenspan is an American economist who served as the 13th chairman of the Federal Reserve from 1987 to 2006. He worked as a private adviser and provided consulting for firms through his company, Greenspan Associates LLC. First nominated to the Federal Reserve by President Ronald Reagan in August 1987, Greenspan was reappointed at successive four-year intervals until retiring on January 31, 2006, after the second-longest tenure in the position, behind only William McChesney Martin.)

Selling Silver Certificates

Misrepresentations: I put this as a separate topic from scams because it can be a different animal. Basically, the point is that you may put your money into a venue and you may not be getting what you think you're buying. A good example is what the respected silver analyst Ted Butler warned about regarding silver certificates. There have been millions of silver certificates issued in recent decades, but there's the real possibility that there isn't any real silver backing them up. In other words, there are purchasers of silver certificates who believe that they could convert their paper into actual silver in due time, but in fact, won't be able to. That sounds like a misrepresentation to me.

FUN FACT:

Just one ounce of gold can actually be physically stretched to a length of 50 miles. The resulting wire would be just five microns wide. - https://www.gold.org/about-gold/gold-facts

What Is the Risk of Being An Emotional Investor?

If you are an emotional person, I personally don't want to spend a lot of time with you because the ups and downs of those mood swings are too jarring to me to be worth it. However, if you are an emotional investor you will lose and lose often. When markets go up and down as they often do you must choose to stay calm and disciplined. You don't want to buy an asset at a high price and sell the asset at a low price.

NOTABLE QUOTABLE

"Be fearful when others are greedy and greedy
when others are fearful."

WARREN BUFFETT

(Warren Edward Buffett is an American investor and philanthropist who is the chairman and former CEO of the conglomerate Berkshire Hathaway. As a result of his success, Buffett is one of the best-known investors in America. According to Forbes, as of January 2026, Buffett's estimated net worth stood at US$148.9 billion, making him the ninth-richest individual in the world. Buffett was born in Omaha, Nebraska. The son of U.S. congressman and businessman Howard Buffett, he developed an interest in business and investing during his youth. He entered the Wharton School of the University of Pennsylvania in 1947, before graduating from the University of Nebraska in Lincoln at 20. He went on to graduate from Columbia Business School, where he molded his investment philosophy around the concept of value investing pioneered by Benjamin Graham.)

What Is the Risk of Being An Impatient Investor?

Most of humanity wants to get rich quickly. However, this is a bad goal for you to have. If you haven't discovered this yet, the quest to make a fast buck typically results in getting poor quickly. People often stretch for quick big gains and they end up with massive losses. When you choose to buy silver and gold and then to hold for the long-term, success is possible. When you choose to buy undervalued real estate and simply wait for the value of the property to go up over time, success is possible.

NOTABLE QUOTABLE

"Wealth gotten by vanity shall be diminished: but
he that gathereth by labour shall increase."

PROVERBS 13:11

*(Proverbs was written by King Solomon. King Solomon became the
world's wealthiest man. However, King Solomon did choose to have
700 wives and 300 concubines. If you are reading this, I would strongly
encourage you to not pursue the goal of finding 700 wives and 300
concubines.)*

When You Sell Gold, Is There a Sales Tax?

When you are selling gold within the United States of America, as a general rule, you will not pay sales tax on the profit. However, you may owe federal gains tax which may be treated as a higher "collectible" rate (max 28%) by the Internal Revenue Service (The IRS). State sales tax rules vary widely with some states actually exempting bullion, but taxing other gold items. As is to be expected, your profit is taxed as short-term (ordinary income) if held under a year, or long-term (collectibles rate) if you decide to hold your gold and silver for over a year. However, these rules change by the state and by the product.

NOTABLE QUOTABLE

"In this world nothing can be said to be certain, except death and taxes."

BENJAMIN FRANKLIN

(Benjamin Franklin (1706 -1790) was the inventor of the skullet hairstyle, an American polymath: a writer, scientist, inventor, statesman, diplomat, printer, publisher and political philosopher. Among the most influential intellectuals of his time, Franklin was one of the Founding Fathers of the United States; a drafter and signer of the Declaration of Independence; and the first postmaster general. Benjamin Franklin invented the first newspaper chain, the lightning rod, the Franklin stove, bifocal glasses and the flexible urinary catheter.)

What Are 100 Taxes That United States Citizens Pay?

In America, you get taxed on your income. Then when you buy something with your remaining income, you get taxed again. Then when you buy an asset, like a home, you get to pay property taxes as a penalty for owning that property each and every year. Thus, in America today, most Americans are now paying far more than 50% of every dollar they earn in taxes. So, as an exciting way to depress you and I both, we have included 101 taxes that most Americans pay and probably love to pay. Yay!

1. Personal / Consumer Taxes & Fees Federal income tax

2. State income tax

3. Local income tax

4. Employee social security tax (your employer pays the other half)

5. Employee Medicare tax (your employer pays the other half)

6. Property taxes

7. Road toll charges

8. State sales tax

9. Driver's license renewal fee

10. TV Cable/Satellite fees & taxes

11. Federal telephone surtax, excise tax, and universal surcharge

12. State telephone excise tax and surcharge

13. Telephone minimum usage and recurring/nonrecurring charges tax

14. Gas/electric bill fees & taxes

15. Water/sewer fees & taxes

16. Cigarette tax

17. Alcohol tax

18. Federal gasoline tax

19. State gasoline tax

20. Local gasoline tax

21. Federal inheritance tax

22. State inheritance tax

23. Gift tax

24. Bridge toll charges

25. Marriage license

26. Hunting license

27. Fishing license

28. Bike license fee

29. Dog permit/license

30. State park permit

31. Watercraft registration & licensing fees

32. Sports stadium tax

33. Bike/nature trail permit

34. Court case filing fee

35. Retirement account early withdrawal penalty

36. Individual health insurance mandate tax

37. Hotel stay tax

38. Plastic surgery surcharge

39. Soda/fatty-food tax

40. Air transportation tax

41. Electronic transmission of tax return fees

42. Passport application/renewal fee

43. Luxury & gas-guzzler car taxes

44. New car surcharge

45. License plate and car ownership transfer taxes

46. Yacht and luxury boat taxes

47. Jewelry taxes & surcharges

48. State/local school tax

49. Recreational vehicle tax

50. Special assessments for road repairs or construction

51. Gun ownership permit

52. Kiddie tax (IRS form 8615)

53. Fuel gross receipts tax

54. Waste Management tax

55. Oil and gas assessment tax

56. Use taxes (on out-of-state purchases)

57. IRA rollover tax/withdrawal penalties

58. Tax on non-qualified health saving account distributions

59. Individual and small business surtax (page 336 of Obamacare)

60. Estimated income tax underpayment penalty

61. Alternative Minimum Tax on income

62. Business Taxes & Fees

63. Federal corporate income tax

64. State corporate income tax

65. Tax registration fee for new businesses

66. Employer social security tax

67. Employer Medicare tax

68. Federal unemployment tax

69. State unemployment tax

70. Business registration renewal tax

71. Worker's compensation tax

72. Tax on imported/exported goods

73. Oil storage/inspection fees

74. Employer health insurance mandate tax

75. Excise Tax on Charitable Hospitals (page 2001/Sec. 9007 of Obamacare)

76. Tax on Innovator Drug Companies (Page 2010/Sec. 9008 of Obamacare)

77. Tax on Medical Device Manufacturers (Page 2020/Sec. 9009 of Obamacare)

78. Tax on Health Insurers (Page 2026/Sec. 9010 of Obamacare)

79. Excise Tax on Comprehensive Health Insurance Plans, i.e., "Cadillac" plans

80. Tax on indoor tanning services

81. Utility users tax

82. Internet transaction fee (passed in California; being considered in other states and at federal level)

83. Professional license fee (accountants, lawyers, barbers, dentists, plumbers, etc.)

84. Franchise business tax

85. Tourism and concession license fee

86. Wiring inspection fees

87. Household employment tax

88. Biodiesel fuel tax

89. FDIC tax (insurance premium on bank deposits)

90. Electronic waste recycling fee

91. Hazardous material disposal fee

92. Food & beverage license fee

93. Estimated income tax underpayment penalty

94. Building/construction permit

95. Zoning permit

96. Fire inspection fee

97. Well permit tax

98. Sales and Use tax seller's permit

99. Commercial driver's license fee

100. Bank ATM transaction tax

101. Occupation taxes and fees (annual charges required for a host of professions)

NOTABLE QUOTABLE

"Because gold is honest money, it is disliked by dishonest men."

RON PAUL

(Ron Paul (born August 20, 1935) is an American author, activist, medical doctor, and former politician who served as the U.S. representative for Texas's 22nd congressional district from 1976 to 1977, and again from 1979 to 1985, as well as for Texas's 14th congressional district from 1997 to 2013. On three occasions, he sought the presidency of the United States, first as the Libertarian Party nominee in 1988, and then as a candidate for the Republican Party in 2008 and 2012.)

NOTABLE QUOTABLE

"A person may not like someone else's religion, but he'll accept his gold."

ROBERT KIYOSAKI

(Robert Kiyosaki is an international best-selling author of the Rich Dad Poor Dad book series, a legendary real estate investor, multiple-time ThrivetimeShow.com podcast guest, and entrepreneur. Kiyosaki is the author of more than 26 books, including the international self-published personal finance Rich Dad Poor Dad series of books which has been translated into 51 languages and sold over 41 million copies worldwide.)

“Global central banks on net in 2014 stopped growing their holdings of treasury bonds and they bought about $600 billion of gold...”

LUKE GROMEN ON THE TUCKER CARLSON SHOW (FEBRUARY 24TH 2025)

Luke Gromen holds a Bachelor of Business Administration degree in finance and accounting from the University of Cincinnati and received his MBA from Case Western Reserve University.

“According to the International Monetary Fund, U.S. dollar reserves held in central banks have fallen to their lowest level in 25 years...The BRICS nations are exploring new reserve currency reportedly called the Unit and backed by gold... The BRICS central banks are buying gold at record levels and are reducing their share of U.S. dollar reserves.”

KITCO NEWS HOSTED BY MICHELLE MAKORI (SEPTEMBER 21ST 2024)

CHAPTER 04

D

Dollars Decrease In Value While Gold & Silver Increase In Value

What Are the Properties of Gold?

Gold is an element found on the standard periodic table of the chemical elements. Gold is listed there with the symbol AU and the atomic number 79. (Don't worry, the quiz has been canceled). Gold is the most malleable and ductile of the metals. You could actually take a single ounce of gold and essentially stretch it out into 300 square feet. (No, I don't know why you would do it, but it sounds impressive). Gold is a good conductor of heat and electricity (and probably thieves as well). Because it's generally resistant to rust and corrosion, gold quickly became an ideal material to fashion with jewelry, coins, and therefore, money. The desirability of gold now became ensured.

NOTABLE QUOTABLE

"When paper money systems begin to crack at the seams, the run to gold could be explosive."

HARRY BROWNE

(Harry Edson Browne (June 17, 1933 – March 1, 2006) was an American writer, libertarian political activist, and investment advisor. He was the Libertarian Party's presidential nominee in the U.S. elections of 1996 and 2000. He authored 12 books that in total have sold more than 2 million copies including his influential work How I Found Freedom in an Unfree World (1973), which provided a blueprint for achieving individual liberation by rejecting societal constraints and embracing self-reliance. In one of the final books that Harry Browne wrote called, Fail-Safe Investing: Lifelong Financial Security In 30 Minutes, he wrote about keeping 25% of your investments in gold. However, you and I are not Harry Browne, and before reading this book you probably didn't know who Harry Browne was.)

Why Is Every Society On the Planet Earth Inflating Their Currency?

NOTABLE QUOTABLE

"Whenever destroyers appear among men, they start by destroying money, for money is men's protection and the base of a moral existence. Destroyers seize gold and leave to its owners a counterfeit pile of paper. This kills all objective standards and delivers men into the arbitrary power of an arbitrary setter of values. Gold was an objective value, an equivalent of wealth produced. Paper is a mortgage on wealth that does not exist, backed by a gun aimed at those who are expected to produce it. Paper is a check drawn by legal looters upon an account which is not theirs: upon the virtue of the victims. Watch for the day when it bounces, marked: "Account Overdrawn."

AYN RAND

(Ayn Rand (1905 – March 6, 1982), better known by her pen name Ayn Rand, was a Russian-American writer and philosopher. She is known for her fiction and for developing a philosophical system which she named Objectivism. Born and educated in Russia, she moved to the United States in 1926. After two early novels that were initially unsuccessful and two Broadway plays, Rand achieved fame with her 1943 novel The Fountainhead. In 1957, she published her best-selling work, the novel Atlas Shrugged. Afterward, until her death in 1982, she turned to non-fiction to promote her philosophy, publishing her own periodicals, and releasing several collections of essays.)

Who is Buying Gold?

- BRICS (Brazil, Russia, India, China & South Africa) nations are buying copious amounts of gold to decrease their reliance on the U.S. dollar and to ultimately create their own global reserve currency that will be backed by gold. The BRICS nations are pushing to diversify their reserves, to create a completely alternative financial system that will allow them to no longer need to view the U.S. dollar as being relevant. This long-term strategy has been executed by the BRICS nations over the past (nearly) twenty years, and this strategy involves increased gold production, and the purchasing of gold from the international market. The BRICS nations are building gold-backed settlements, with China, Russia, and India leading the accumulation of the gold effort. Some experts now believe that the BRICS nations now control the majority of global reserves.

- Central banks have been continuing to buy massive amounts of gold to diversify their reserves and to also reduce their dependency on the U.S. dollar. As of 2026, Gold has now overtaken the euro to become the second-largest reserve asset globally, trailing only the U.S. dollar. As geopolitical risks and turmoil increase throughout the world, Central Banks continue to buy more and more gold. Central banks are increasingly moving away from the dollar and they are choosing to invest in gold.

- Informed investors and people that want to protect their wealth against inflation are choosing to buy silver and gold. Gold buying is no longer reserved for people that choose to live underground year-round in a bunker to protect themselves from "the attack of the commies." Gold and silver buying is no longer an investment strategy reserved for the "preppers" only. For years many believed that only "preppers" who were stockpiling goods in preparation for an end times doomsday situation were investing in gold and silver. When the world's leading financial experts such as Ray Dalio, and the world's leading entrepreneurial authors such as Robert Kiyosaki, are encouraging people to buy gold to protect against inflation, you know that gold has gone mainstream. When the entire BRICS (Brazil, Russia, India, China, South Africa) alliance of countries is openly stating that their plan is to stockpile the earth's gold in preparation to "de-dollarize" and to introduce a new gold-backed reserve currency, you and I can rest assured that the value of gold is going to keep going up and up as the value of the U.S. dollar continues to go down and down.

NOTABLE QUOTABLE

""A prohibition on the hoarding or possession
of gold was integral to the plan to devalue the
dollar against gold and get people spending again.
Against this background, FDR issued Executive
Order 6102 on April 5, 1933, one of the most
extraordinary executive orders in U.S. history.
The blunt language over the signature of Franklin
Delano Roosevelt speaks for itself: I, Franklin D.
Roosevelt . . . declare that [a] national emergency
still continues to exist and . . . do hereby prohibit
the hoarding of gold coin, gold bullion, and
gold certificates within the . . . United States
by individuals, partnerships, associations and
corporations.... All persons are hereby required
to deliver, on or before May 1, 1933, to a Federal
reserve bank . . . or to any member of the Federal
Reserve System all gold coin, gold bullion and
gold certificates now owned by them.... Whoever
willfully violates any provision of this Executive
Order . . . may be fined not more than $10,000

or . . . may be imprisoned for not more than ten years. The people of the United States were being ordered to surrender their gold to the government and were offered paper money at the exchange rate of $20.67 per ounce. Some relatively minor exceptions were made for dentists, jewelers and others who made "legitimate and customary" use of gold in their industry or art. Citizens were allowed to keep $100 worth of gold, about five ounces at 1933 prices, and gold in the form of rare coins. The $10,000 fine proposed in 1933 for those who continued to hoard gold in violation of the president's order is equivalent to over $165,000 in today's money, an extraordinarily large statutory fine."

JAMES G. RICKARDS,

CURRENCY WARS: THE MAKING OF THE NEXT GLOBAL CRISIS

(James G. Rickards is an American lawyer, economist, investment banker, speaker, media commentator, and author on matters of finance and precious metals. He graduated from Johns Hopkins University in 1973 with a Bachelor of Arts degree with honors, and in 1974, from the Paul H. Nitze School of Advanced International Studies in Washington, D.C., with an M.A. in international economics. He received his Juris Doctor from the University of Pennsylvania Law School and a Master of Laws in taxation from New York University School of Law. He has held senior positions at Citibank, Long-Term Capital Management, and Caxton Associates. Rickards worked on Wall Street for 35 years.)

Is Silver Similar to Gold?

Silver is very similar to gold in many ways including:

- Both silver and gold have been viewed as an acceptable form of money since ancient times.

- Silver is not synthetic. Silver is not man-made and it must be mined out of the ground.

- Because the total world supply for silver is limited based upon the ability of humans to mine it, silver has a finite supply.

- Both silver and gold are found under the ground, so we do not know how much silver and gold exists in total.

- There is a finite amount of both gold and silver that can be mined. At some point in the future (if Christ doesn't return first), we will reach a point where no more silver and gold can be found because we have mined it all.

What Is the Purpose of Silver Bars And Ingots?

When purchasing silver to protect your wealth, most buyers choose to buy silver bars, ingots, or silver coins. If your goal is to get the maximum amount of silver metal for the purchase price, bullion bars are a great way to go. If you are looking to purchase silver bars that are really small, you may want to consider buying ingots because ingots are small metal bars and they are fun to say.

Try saying ingots five times this week to your family and friends to impress them and yourselves with your vast and newfound knowledge of all things gold and silver. Ingots can be described as being small bars that often come imprinted with various marks and designs to make the bars more attractive, unique, and collectable. As a word of caution, ingots are typically desired by collectors of precious metals more than investors in the actual metal of silver.

What Is the Difference Between Owning Physical Gold And Silver Or Paper Gold And Silver?

When you have physical ownership of your gold and silver, this means that you own a real tangible physical asset which you have access to. When you invest in gold and silver paper (certificates), this is not a good thing. When you own a paper asset, this simply means that you have a claim to an asset via a piece of paper that was issued to you that guarantees you have a claim to this asset. However, many of the organizations that sell these "claims" to physical pieces of gold and silver have no problem with selling "claims" to the same piece of gold and silver multiple times over. Imagine a real estate agent sold your house to 10 buyers and hoped that none of the buyers would ever actually move into the new home they purchased. This is what it is like to invest in gold and silver paper, claims, and certificates.

Does Gold Purity Matter When Investing In Gold And Silver?

If you were to buy 100% pure gold, it would be too soft for regular use. This gold needs to be hardened in order for it to have a practical use. Gold is alloyed (mixed with other metals such as copper or silver or another metal) to make it suitable for everyday and industrial use. As an example, twenty-four-karat jewelry must be handled with extreme care, rather than 14-karat gold because the gold in 24-karat gold is much more malleable and soft.

Want to Know More About Gold Karats?

- **24-karat gold:** This is pure gold (100% gold)

- **22-karat gold:** This is 11/12 gold and 1/12 other (such as copper). When you invest in buying a bullion coin or bar that is described as being 22-karat gold, this is roughly 92% pure gold.

- **18-karat gold:** This is 18/24 gold (the other 6/24 is copper or other metal). This means that approximately 75% of the physical item you are purchasing is pure gold.

- **14-karat gold:** This means that 14/24 of the item is actually gold. In other words, 58.3% of the item you are purchasing is pure gold.

What Is the Most Commonly Used Gold In the United States Jewelry Industry?

14-karat (14K) gold is currently the most popular type of gold that is used within the United States jewelry industry. 14-karat gold is commonly used for engagement rings and everyday jewelry because it is affordable and durable. At a 58.3% gold content, most consumers still appreciate the color of 14-karat gold while also appreciating its durability. Although much less common than 14-karat gold, 18-karat gold is typically used for luxury jewelry pieces. As a note, 10-karat gold is the legal minimum for gold jewelry in the United States. If you are buying 9-karat gold jewelry, buying Coach purses from a sidewalk / street vendor in New York City or corresponding via email with a "Saudi Prince" who wants you to invest in his fast-growth high-tech startup there is a high probability that you are getting scammed.

Want to Know More About Carrots?

The vegetables that we now describe as carrots are believed to have originated over 5,000 years ago in Central Asia, specifically around modern-day Afghanistan and Iran. These purple, yellow, or white root vegetables were first used more for their leaves and seeds than for the roots themselves. However, the horses at my ranch love eating carrots (the roots), and they do not seem interested in the carrot leaves. Carrots were spread to the Mediterranean and then to Europe. As the good news of carrots spread throughout the Mediterranean and Europe, the orange carrot that we now enjoy and eat today was developed by those always industrious Dutch farmers around the 17th century through a process of selective breeding as a very intentional plan to pay a patriotic tribute to the House of Orange. The House of Orange-

Nassau is also known as the Dutch royal family. This family was named after the medieval Principality of Orange, and has been central to Dutch history since William the Silent led the revolt against Spain in the 16th century.

NOTABLE QUOTABLE

"If you have faith in our leaders of commerce, don't buy gold. If you do not have faith in them, maybe you should buy gold or silver."

ROBERT KIYOSAKI

(Robert Kiyosaki is an international best-selling author of the Rich Dad Poor Dad book series, a legendary real estate investor, multiple-time ThrivetimeShow.com podcast guest, and entrepreneur. Kiyosaki is the author of more than 26 books, including the international self-published personal finance Rich Dad Poor Dad series of books which has been translated into 51 languages and sold over 41 million copies worldwide.)

What Is the Best Way to Actually Buy Gold And Silver?

If you are looking to invest in the purchasing of gold and silver, you need to look into investing in the purchasing of actual physical gold and silver. When you contact a dealer to buy gold and silver make sure that you are receiving actual gold and silver and not a gold and silver certificate.

What Is Your Break-Even Point?

How Much Does the Price of Gold or Silver Need to Increase for You to Break-Even On Your Investment In Gold or Silver (After Commissions, Fees, Taxes, Etc.)?

After paying all of the fees and really doing all of the math...If I buy this much gold and silver, how much would the price of gold and silver need to go up in value for me to be able to generate a profit based upon the gold and silver that I am buying?

Should You Buy Gold Or Silver?

When you decide to purchase gold and silver you must sit down and do that hard math. Ask yourself the following questions:

1. If I buy this much gold and silver, how much would the price of gold and silver need to go up in value for me to be able to generate a profit based upon the gold and silver that I am buying?

2. After fees...if I buy this much gold and silver, how much would the price of gold and silver need to go up in value for me to be able to generate a profit based upon the gold and silver that I am buying?

What Does the Process of Transferring Your IRA to Gold Look Like?

If you want to transfer your Individual Retirement Account (IRA) to gold, you must open a special Self-Directed IRA (SDIRA), which involves using a custodian that handles precious metals. This custodian will then assist you in initiating a tax-free direct rollover or transfer from your old IRA (Individual Retirement Account), allowing the new custodian to buy IRS-approved physical gold (bars or coins) for secure storage in an approved depository, not your possession. However, if you choose to take physical possession of the silver and gold rather than choosing to hold your silver and gold with a custodian then you are going to pay taxes. The process of transferring your IRA into gold involves first selecting a precious metals dealer you can trust, doing the paperwork, funding the new account, selecting the approved metals, and arranging for secure, IRS-compliant storage.

NOTABLE QUOTABLE

"I like gold because it is a stabilizer; it is an insurance policy."

KEVIN O'LEARY

(Terrence Thomas Kevin O'Leary (born July 9, 1954), also known as Mr. Wonderful, is a Canadian businessman, television personality, and actor. From 2004 to 2014, he appeared on various Canadian television shows, including the business news program The Lang and O'Leary Exchange as well as reality television shows Dragons' Den and Redemption Inc. O'Leary hosted Discovery Channel's Project Earth in 2008 and has appeared on Shark Tank, the American version of Dragons' Den, since 2009. He made his feature film debut as Milton Rockwell in Josh Safdie's Marty Supreme (2025).)

What Do I Need to Know About Gold IRAs?

As a general rule, if you choose to hold precious metals inside of an IRA (Individual Retirement Account), you must have a custodian (which is most commonly a trust company) which will administer over the account to make sure that your account is in compliance with the various laws and tax laws.

This custodian is required to work with a depository where the physical metals are sent after the purchase has occurred until you decide to either liquidate your gold and silver for cash or you decide to take physical possession / distribution of the gold and silver (this is also known as an in- kind distribution) and to make this sentence longer I have added addition unnecessary words.

My friend, if you do decide to actually take possession of the gold and silver that you just bought, this is considered to be a distribution, which will cause you to pay taxes because this is a taxable event. Yay! I love paying taxes and I know that you do too! So...DOUBLE YAY!!! However, as a quick note...you can sell your gold and silver within your IRA (Individual Retirement Account) and decide to keep the proceeds as cash in your account without actually triggering a taxable event and the paying of taxes. Are you confused yet? Remember, there are no bad students, there are just bad teachers.

Where Should You Store Your Gold?

I would not recommend telling the folks at your favorite local bar where you are storing your gold. I would not recommend telling your nefarious brother-in-law where you are storing your gold. Think about it for a second? Where is a secure place where you could store your silver and gold? If you store your gold in a vault that is administered by a custodian somewhere, you probably can't get it if the communists invade America. However, if the communists physically invade America, you probably are going to wish you would have invested more in lead and less in gold.

What Happens If Western Civilization Ends And You Need Your Gold And Silver to Give You Access to Your Gold?

If you read Revelation Chapter 16:12-14, Revelation Chapter 18:21-23, Mark Chapter 13, Luke Chapter 21, Matthew Chapter 24, Daniel Chapter 2 and Daniel Chapter 4, you would probably be very concerned about the current state of the world, and would probably be very aware that the Biblical prophecy is coming to pass. You then might be worried about the end of Western Civilization and the collapse of the banking systems (Revelation Chapter 6:6). Thus, if you are sincerely concerned about humanity approaching the end of the age, you may also want to think about investing in lead as part of a balanced precious metal portfolio in addition to the stockpiling of gold and silver.

What are the Important Terms, Definitions And Phrases That You Should Know About When Investing In Gold?

Before you go out and buy gold and silver, we believe that you need to at least be familiar with the following key definitions:

Ask Price - The ask price for gold is in reference to the lowest price a seller (like a dealer or market maker) is willing to accept to sell a unit of gold. While buyers pay this price when purchasing; it's always higher than the bid price (what buyers offer), and represents the cost to acquire gold, with the difference (the bid-ask spread) indicating market liquidity and transaction costs. In terms of gold and silver, dealers are in business to make a profit. When you buy gold, you pay the ask price; when you sell, you receive the bid price, and this spread is how dealers profit.

Buy-Back - The gold buy-back is the process of selling gold products that you have previously purchased back to a dealer, jeweler, or financial institution in exchange for cash. The amount that a dealer is willing to buy-back your gold and silver is often related to the weight of the item, the purity of the item, and the current market prices for the gold and silver items you are looking to sell back to the dealer.

Bullion - Bullion gold and silver are precious metals that have been refined to the highest possible purity (typically 99.5% or more) and then formed into standardized bars, ingots, or coins. For a good time, try using the word ingot in a sentence with your friends and family. Bullion is valued primarily based upon the metal content rather than numismatic appeal. Again, numismatic coins are in reference to collectable, rare, premium and hard-to-find coins. Bullion gold and silver has proven over time to be a good wealth store during economic uncertainty. Key attributes of gold and silver bullion include their high purity (e.g., .999 fine), standardized weight, and their unique status as being physical assets, with gold often requiring 99.9% purity and silver 99.99% for certain investments like IRAs (An Individual Retirement Accounts) to recognize them. "Bullion" is the industry term or a fancy word for a raw metal. Bullion metal is often sold in the form of a bar, ingot, or a standardized coin.

CASH IRA Distribution - An IRA cash distribution is basically a withdrawal of money (cash) from your Individual Retirement Account. This withdrawal of money is sent directly to you via check, ACH, or wire, as opposed to an "in-kind" distribution of assets like stocks. Although you can take cash anytime, these withdrawals from your Individual Retirement Account are usually taxable as ordinary income and may incur a 10% early withdrawal penalty if you're under 59½, unless an exception applies, with specific rules for Roth IRAs and Required Minimum Distributions (RMDs) starting at age 73.

Conservative Investor - A conservative investor is a person that seeks to invest in quality investments (such as gold, silver, and stocks that have proven, solid and good fundamentals) to hold onto for the long-term. Conservative investors work hard to avoid short-term guess-work style investing and speculative trading.

Custodian (IRA) - An IRA custodian is a financial institution (which could be a bank or a trust company) that is legally required to hold and administer your

Individual Retirement Account. An IRA custodian is responsible for safeguarding your assets and ensuring that compliance is occurring with the current IRS rules, processing transactions, and handling required reporting (like forms 1099-R and 5498) in order to maintain the account's tax-advantaged status. An IRA custodian acts as a passive record-keeper for your investments and is responsible for handling the administrative details so you are able to save for retirement.

Custodial Engineer - A janitor. A person who is typically responsible for the general upkeep and maintenance of a building, office, or school.

Dealer Premium / Mark-Up - A dealer premium/markup on gold is that extra cost above the spot price (current market value) that dealers charge to cover the costs of running their dealership including marketing, manufacturing, refining, shipping, administrative costs, overhead, and more. While bullion bars might have the lowest premiums in the marketplace (1-3%) jewelry often has the highest markups (often 50-475%). When precious companies decide to create an exclusive or premium coin, they don't literally mint the coin themselves. Precious metals companies work with a well-known and reputable mint who will (for an agreed-upon fee) create / mint coins according to the client's specifications. The relationship is 100% legit and is perfectly legal. Although national mints are connected to the United States government, many choose to also operate as though they were a private and individually-held business or corporation. Thus, they operate-for-profit business.

However, you must know, the U.S. Mint does fall under the Department of the Treasury, which makes it an official government agency. However, in Canada, our neighbors to the north, The Royal Canadian Mint, is also connected with the Canadian government, but much more casually. The Royal Canadian Mint is known as a "Crown Corporation." This means that The Royal Canadian Mint has responsibilities to the government, and it receives oversight from the state government, however it is allowed to engage in private business as long as the mint is able to keep up with its core duties to the Canadian government.

Exclusive / Premium Coins - Typically exclusive and premium gold coins are high-purity, and meticulously crafted gold coins with detailed intricate designs, limited mintages, and special finishes (like proof). Exclusive / premium coins are unlike bullion coins which are solely based on metal content.

Golden Look - This is a marketing term that Clay Clark uses to describe the moment when your ideal and likely buyer considers hiring your service or buying your product as a result of your compelling marketing, powerful calls to action, and your world-class branding.

Goldmember - Goldmember is a fictitious character created for the Austin Powers movie series starring Mike Meyers. Goldmember is called Goldmember because he's obsessed with gold, even coating his body in it and losing his genitalia in a "smelting accident," leading to his name which is a pun on the villain from the classic James Bond film Goldfinger. The character, a Dutch villain in the Austin Powers series, loves gold so much he eats his own dead skin, wears gold, and refers to himself as "Goldmember," a play on the Bond villain Auric Goldfinger.

Gold-Plated Diapers - "Babies.. before we're done here.. y'all be wearing gold-plated diapers." - Bruce Dickinson (A fictional music producer from a Saturday Night Live Skit called "More Cowbell"). "More Cowbell" is a comedy sketch that aired on Saturday Night Live on April 8, 2000. The sketch was written by regular cast member Will Ferrell and depicts the recording of the song "(Don't Fear) The Reaper" by Blue Öyster Cult. The sketch stars guest host Christopher Walken as fictional music producer Bruce Dickinson, and Ferrell as fictional cowbell player Gene Frenkle, whose overzealous playing annoys his bandmates but pleases Dickinson. The sketch also features Chris Parnell as Eric Bloom, Jimmy Fallon as Bobby Rondinelli, Chris Kattan as Buck Dharma, and Horatio Sanz as Joe Bouchard.

In-Kind IRA Distribution - An in-kind IRA distribution is in reference to the action of taking actual investments (like stocks, bonds, or ETFs) out of your retirement account and moving those investments into a taxable brokerage account, instead of cashing them out first. By doing this, this allows you to avoid selling assets within the IRA, and to maintain your investment position. This move allows you to potentially benefit from lower future capital gains taxes and meet obligations like Required Minimum Distributions (RMDs) without forced liquidation. However, the fair market value of the distributed assets is still taxed as ordinary income. If this concept blows your mind, please talk to your precious metals expert of choice for added clarity. Just typing this definition made me dizzy and quasi-nauseous.

Junk Silver - The phrase "Junk Silver" is used in reference to pre-1965 U.S. dimes, quarters, and half-dollars which were actually and incredibly minted with 90% silver. The value of these pre-1965 U.S. dimes, quarters and half-dollars is strictly based upon their metal content and not on their "collector / numismatic" value. "Junk Silver" is very popular and affordable because it is a simple and divisible way to buy silver. "Junk Silver" is bought and sold simply based upon their "melt" value. Melt value is totally based upon the intrinsic worth of a physical item such as bullion, coins, or jewelry and is based solely on the current market price of the precious metals that are contained. Melt value completely ignores any value related to "collectors / numismatic" value. Melt value is not based upon the craftsmanship, the detail, the uniqueness or the rarity of the item. I BELIEVE THAT BUYING JUNK SILVER IS AN INCREDIBLY SMART INVESTMENT IF YOU ARE LOOKING TO ACQUIRE GOLD AND SILVER FOR ITS MELT VALUE. I BELIEVE GETTING A TATTOO ON YOUR FACE IS AN INVESTMENT WORTH THINKING ABOUT TWICE BEFORE TAKING ACTION.

Karats - Karat (K) is a unit that has been created to measure the purity of a gold item. 24 karat gold is 100% pure, while lower numbers like 14 karat or 18 karat gold indicates that other metals (like silver, copper) have been mixed with the gold for added strength and durability, which makes gold suitable for everyday jewelry.

Melt Value - The melt value is the actual intrinsic worth of an item, such as a piece of jewelry or a coin, based strictly and purely on the weight and current market price (spot price) of the precious metal it contains (gold, silver, platinum). Melt value ignores any numismatic or collectible value.

Numismatic Coins - Numismatics refers to coin collecting. According to the good folks Merriam-Webster, the term Numismatics means, "the study or collection of coins, tokens, and paper money and sometimes related objects (such as medals)." My friend, numismatics is the study or collection of coins, various paper currency, limited edition coins, medals, and hard-to-find coins. When investing in gold to protect your wealth, you want to make sure that you are investing in actual physical gold and silver. When investing in gold and silver, you must be thinking about what the gold and silver would actually be worth in the event that you wanted to sell the gold and silver tomorrow.

Spot Price - The spot price of gold is the most current and real-time market price for immediate purchase or sale of gold. The spot price of gold is typically quoted via U.S. dollars per troy ounce. The spot price of gold is related to global supply and demand in over-the-counter (OTC) markets like COMEX. The COMEX (Commodity Exchange Inc.) is the world's leading derivatives exchange for trading futures and options contracts on metals, including gold, silver, copper, and aluminum. COMEX was founded in 1933 and is now part of the CME Group, based in New York. It serves as a primary hub for global price discovery and risk management in the metals market.

Spread - The "spread" as it relates to the buying and selling of gold is in reference to the bid-ask spread, which is the difference between the highest price a buyer is willing to pay (bid) and the lowest price that a seller will accept (ask) for gold. The spread represents a dealer's profit.

The Golden Baby - This is a term that only Clay Clark uses. Clay Clark uses this term to refer to any new employee that might grow up to become an all-star after enough mentoring and coaching.

The Golden Rule - The Golden Rule is the principle of treating others as one would want to be treated by them. It is sometimes called an ethics of reciprocity, meaning that one should reciprocate to others how one would like them to treat the person (not necessarily how they actually treat them). Matthew 7:12 from the Bible states, "Therefore all things whatsoever ye would that men should do to you, do ye even so to them: for this is the law and the prophets."

Troy Ounce - Gold and silver are measured in troy ounces. The regular weight that you and I might use to weigh ourselves is different from troy ounces. You and I typically weigh things using a measurement referred to as avoirdupois. Try using the phrase avoirdupois around your friends and family this week and see how it goes. The troy ounce is approximately 10 percent heavier than an avoirdupois equivalent. Thus, when you are buying bullion coins and bars, they are typically bought and sold based upon the metal content and almost nothing else. Thus, make sure that when you are buying gold and silver that you are paying for and receiving troy ounces.

NOTABLE QUOTABLE

"The rise in the price of gold is a sign that
capitalism has stumbled."

ROBERT KIYOSAKI

*(Robert Kiyosaki is an international best-selling author of the Rich Dad
Poor Dad book series, a legendary real estate investor, multiple-time
ThrivetimeShow.com podcast guest, and entrepreneur. Kiyosaki is the
author of more than 26 books, including the international self-published
personal finance Rich Dad Poor Dad series of books which has been
translated into 51 languages and sold over 41 million copies worldwide.)*

What Are the Known Properties of Gold?

Gold is an element that can be located on the standard periodic
table of the chemical elements that you and I love to casually read
so much. Gold is listed on the periodic table under the symbol AU
and has the unique atomic number of 79. Gold is considered to be
the most malleable and ductile of the metals. Gold is an incredible
conductor of heat and an incredible conductor of electricity. Gold
is generally thought to be resistant to the process of rusting and
to corrosion; thus over time gold grew to become known as a
perfect material to turn into jewelry, to mint into coins, and to be
used as money.

What Is the Risk of Buying Gold And Deciding to Hold?

In order to achieve the best investment gain possible, it would make logical sense to buy gold and hold. Holding the gold for a long period of time would allow an adequate time for the gold to appreciate in value and for the United States dollar to lose value. However, there is a strong possibility that you will experience death, and when you are dead, it would be very hard for you to experience the upside of owning and holding gold over time. Thus, I would recommend that you buy and hold gold, but I would eventually sell before you get too old to enjoy the benefits of being a smart investor.

NOTABLE QUOTABLE

"Gold has intrinsic value. The problem with the
dollar is it has no intrinsic value. And if the Federal
Reserve is going to spend trillions of them to buy
up all these bad mortgages and all other kinds of
bad debt, the dollar is going to lose all of its value.
Gold will store its value, and you'll always be able
to buy more food with your gold."

PETER SCHIFF

(Peter David Schiff is an American stockbroker, financial commentator, and radio personality. He co-founded Echelon Wealth Partners in Canada (formerly Euro Pacific Canada). He is involved in other financial services companies including Euro Pacific Asset Management, as an independent investment advisor, and Schiff Gold (formerly Euro Pacific Precious Metals). He has criticized US banking and credit practices.)

What Are Essential and Must Read Recommended Books That You Should Read If You Want to Learn More About Investing In Gold And Silver?

- *The Collapse of the Dollar and How to Profit from It: Make a Fortune by Investing in Gold and Other Hard Assets* by James Turk

- *Investing in Gold & Silver For Dummies* by Paul Mladjenovic (Author)

- *The Creature from Jekyll Island: A Second Look at the Federal Reserve* by G. Edward Griffin

- *Rich Dad's Guide to Investing: What the Rich Invest in, That the Poor and the Middle Class Do Not!* by Robert Kiyosaki

- *Rich Dad Poor Dad: What the Rich Teach Their Kids About Money That the Poor and Middle Class Do Not!* by Robert Kiyosaki

"Central banks and finance ministries do not hold copper, aluminum, or steel supplies, yet they hold gold. The only explanation for central bank gold hoards is the obvious one - gold is money."

JAMES G. RICKARDS, CURRENCY WARS: THE MAKING OF THE NEXT GLOBAL CRISIS

James G. Rickards is an American lawyer, economist, investment banker, speaker, media commentator, and author on matters of finance and precious metals. He graduated from Johns Hopkins University in 1973 with a Bachelor of Arts degree with honors, and in 1974, from the Paul H. Nitze School of Advanced International Studies in Washington, D.C., with an M.A. in international economics. He received his Juris Doctor from the University of Pennsylvania Law School and a Master of Laws in taxation from New York University School of Law. He has held senior positions at Citibank, Long-Term Capital Management, and Caxton Associates. Rickards worked on Wall Street for 35 years.)

NOTABLE QUOTABLE

Is Gold & Silver God's Money? "The silver is mine, and the gold is mine, saith the Lord of hosts."

HAGGAI 2:8

(The Book of Haggai was believed to be written by a prophet by the name of Haggai around 520 B.C. to push the Jewish remnant to finish and complete the rebuilding of the Temple in Jerusalem after they returned from their Babylonian exile.)

How Liquid (Easy to Convert Into Cash) Is Gold?

- When you decide to invest in precious metals you must understand that you are not investing in securities, you are investing in physical commodities. When you buy gold and silver you are buying a physical metal that has both monetary value and industrial value, however your gold and silver is not worth anything unless somebody else wants to buy it. Think about it this way.

- When you own a house and it is 100% paid for, you could also simultaneously be broke and without cash unless somebody else wants to buy your house.

- When you put your house on the market and decide to sell your house, you will not have any actual cash unless somebody decides to buy your house.

- When you decide to sell your house, this process may often take 6 months or more before you find a buyer who is willing to buy your house.

- When you decide to sell your house, the buyer who wants to buy your house may not want to pay you what your house is worth.

- When you buy gold and silver you can typically find a dealer that is willing to buy your gold and silver and to pay you with cash within 5 days at an internationally recognized price.

- I cannot think of a single investment that is more liquid than gold and silver.

What Are Securities?

Securities are fungible, tradable financial instruments used to raise capital in public and private markets, representing either ownership (stocks), a creditor relationship (bonds), or rights to ownership (derivatives). Securities hold a monetary value and are heavily regulated to ensure accurate information for investors, with common examples including shares, debentures, and notes.

When It Comes to Buying and Investing In Gold What Do You Need to Remember?

G - Gold and Silver protect your wealth because they have both monetary and industrial value.

O - Owning gold and silver allows you to have tangible assets that do not have counterparty risks.

L - Liquid assets such as gold allow you to be financially malleable.

D - Dollars decrease in value while gold and silver increase in value.

Should You View Investing In Gold As Insurance?

When you decide to invest in owning physical gold, you are investing in storing wealth, minimizing your risk, and maintaining liquidity with your assets. Investing in gold is not something that you should be doing if you are looking to strike it rich, to get-rich-quick or to make overnight money.

When the dollar really starts to slide, and panicked bond investors push interest rates back into double digits, people who have bought overpriced homes with adjustable rate mortgages will respond in one of two ways: they'll cut back on everything else in order to make their mortgage payments, or they'll stop making their mortgage payments. Financially strapped home owners will try to sell their homes and, in utter desperation, will take whatever is offered. Home prices will plunge in formerly hot markets, pulling local economies down with them – which in turn will make local homes even less desirable. The result could be very ugly indeed in currently overheated markets like California and Boston. How ugly? In mid 2003, John Templeton, one of the most successful, global money managers of the past half – century, was asked about housing in an interview, his response: "After home prices go down to one-tenth of the highest price homeowners paid, then buy."

NOTABLE QUOTABLE

"We simply attempt to be fearful when others are greedy and to be greedy only when others are fearful."

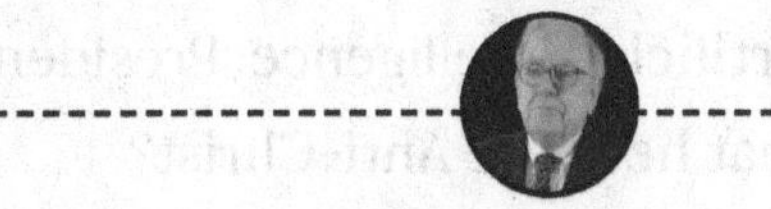

WARREN BUFFET

(Warren Edward Buffett is an American investor and philanthropist who is the chairman and former CEO of the conglomerate Berkshire Hathaway. As a result of his success, Buffett is one of the best-known investors in the world. According to Forbes, as of January 2026, Buffett's estimated net worth stood at US$148.9 billion, making him the ninth-richest person in the world. The companies that are owned by Warren Buffet's Berkshire Hathaway are often household names. In fact, the massive conglomerate (Berkshire Hathaway) holding company led by Warren Buffett now owns numerous subsidiaries outright and holds significant, controlling stakes in major public companies: Key wholly-owned subsidiaries include GEICO, BNSF Railway, Berkshire Hathaway Energy, Dairy Queen, NetJets, Lubrizol, and Fruit of the Loom. Its massive investment portfolio is dominated by large equity stakes in Apple, American Express, Bank of America, Coca-Cola, and Chevron.)

What Will the Government Do With the Gold Being Held By United States Citizens?

1. Will the government decide to freeze the price of gold like it did under President Richard Nixon?

2. Will the United States confiscate the gold of its citizens like it did under the Presidency of Franklin Delano Roosevelt?

3. Will the government introduce programmable money (such as Central Bank Digital Currencies) that can be turned off, turned on and deleted?

4. Will a future artificial intelligence President unzip his face to reveal that he is the Anti-Christ?

The United States government infamously decided to seize the gold held by American citizens through Executive Order 6102, which was signed by the socialist-leaning President Franklin D. Roosevelt on April 5, 1933. The signing of this executive order made it illegal to "hoard" gold coins, bullion, or certificates. This executive order forced private gold owners to turn in their gold to the Federal Reserve in exchange for fiat (currency issued via decree) / paper currency at a fixed rate of $20.67 per ounce. For reasons that do not make sense to most experts as of 2025, the United States Government still officially values its gold reserves at $42.22 per fine troy ounce.

Andrew Sorchini and his wife Lin spend time with General Flynn backstage at Clay Clark's ReAwaken America Tour featuring General Flynn, Eric Trump, Donald J. Trump Jr., Peter Navarro, Alina Habba, Kash Patel, Devin Nunes, Robert F. Kennedy Jr., and many of America's conservative experts and leaders.